COSTA RICA
SPANISH
PHRASEBOOK

Thomas B. Kohnstamm

Costa Rica Spanish phrasebook
1st edition – July 2000

Published by
Lonely Planet Publications Pty Ltd A.C.N. 005 607 983
192 Burwood Rd, Hawthorn, Victoria 3122, Australia

Lonely Planet Offices
Australia PO Box 617, Hawthorn, Victoria 3122
USA 150 Linden St, Oakland CA 94607
UK 10a Spring Place, London NW5 3BH
France 1 rue du Dahomey, 75011 Paris

Cover illustration
Islands in the Stream by Brendan Dempsey

ISBN 1 86450 105 7

text © Lonely Planet Publications 2000
cover illustration © Lonely Planet 2000

Printed by Colorcraft Ltd, Hong Kong

About the Author

Thomas B. Kohnstamm was born and raised in Seattle. He started traveling at the age of 13. Now, a decade later, he is a full-time traveler, part-time skier and surfer, and working is his side hobby.

From the Author

The author wishes to thank his parents Ed and Linda for their unwaivering love and support and for introducing him to the beauty of travel, his brother and friends (you know who you are) for their friendship, Yens for his Costa Rican expertise, his Spanish teachers and professors, and last but not least the unique and amazing people of Costa Rica. Tuanis ma'es.

From the Publisher

This book was developed from Lonely Planet's *Latin American Spanish phrasebook*. Vicki Webb edited and Karin Vidstrup Monk co-edited and proofread. Jo Adams was responsible for layout and design, Patrick Marris for the illustrations on pages 103, 130 and 134, while Penelope Richardson drew all other illustrations. Brendan Dempsey drew the cover illustration, and Natasha Velleley produced the map.

CONTENTS

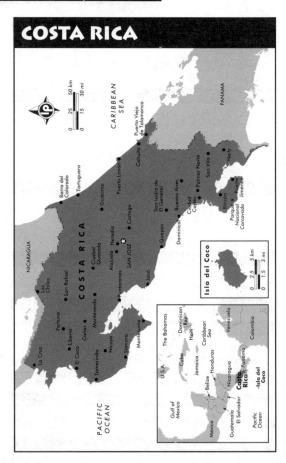

INTRODUCTION

Due to its great ecological diversity, pleasant climate, variety of activities, stable politics and friendly people, Costa Rica is fast becoming one of the most popular travel destinations in Latin America. As the number of foreigners travelling to this small nation increases, it's important that visitors respect the local culture. By attempting to speak Spanish, especially the local dialect, you'll have the opportunity to experience the beauty of Costa Rican culture, and not just use the country as a playground. This phrasebook is a tool for opening doors between you and the warmth and friendliness of the Costa Rican people.

Spanish is one of the most widely spoken languages in the world. Widespread colonisation by Spain in the 16th and 17th centuries ensured Spanish became the predominant language throughout 19 countries on the American continent and in the Caribbean. However, just as the cultures and nations of Latin America didn't develop in a uniform way, the Spanish language now varies from country to country.

Language reflects culture, and the tone of Costa Rican Spanish, like the people of the country, is straightforward and up-beat yet relaxed. The language is relatively informal, yet polite and peppered with colourful, friendly sayings. **Pura Vida** is a very popular saying which characterizes Costa Rican life well. Literally translated as 'pure life', it's really a more profound concept which expresses the positive attitude of the Costa Rican experience.

Costa Ricans are as fascinated by foreigners and their background as you may be with Costa Rican culture and lifestyles. It isn't unusual to be plied with questions when meeting someone for the first time, and any effort to reply in Spanish will be appreciated. For those who already speak Spanish, this phrasebook will help tailor your speech to the local dialect. Good luck and ¡**Pura Vida**!

GETTING STARTED

So you'll always have something to say, you should memorise a few basic words of Spanish. 'Yes' is **sí** and 'no' is **no** – that's easy. A general 'hello' is **hola** (pronounced without the 'h' and a general 'How are you?' is **¿Cómo está?** **Por favor** means 'Please'. It's a good idea to tack this word onto any request you make. 'Thank you' is **Gracias**.

Good luck with your attempts to speak the language or, as they say in Costa Rica, **¡Buena suerte!**

ARTHUR OR MARTHA?

Spanish has two noun forms, known as masculine and feminine (see page 13 in Grammar). In this book, the feminine form is placed first, and the masculine second.

It should be noted that any mixed group of masculine and feminine objects or people take the masculine form. A group of male (**niños**) and female (**niñas**) children are simply called **niños**. The group wouldn't be called **niñas** unless it was entirely female.

In this book, feminine (-a) and masculine (-o) endings are separated by a slash:

    musician   **música/o**

When a definite article precedes a noun, both feminine and masculine forms of the article are given in full:

    the photographer   **la/el fotógrafa/o**

When the feminine form of a word is formed by adding -a to the masculine form, -a is given in parentheses.

    a curator   **un(a) conservador(a)**

ABBREVIATIONS USED IN THIS BOOK

adj	adjective	n	noun
col	colloquial usage	pl	plural
f	feminine	pol	polite
inf	informal	sg	singular
lit	literally	vulg	vulgar
m	masculine		

PRONUNCIATION

Spanish pronunciation isn't difficult – there's a clear and consistent relationship between pronunciation and spelling, and English speakers will find that many Spanish sounds are similar to their English counterparts. If you stick to the following rules you should have very few problems being understood.

VOWELS

Unlike English, each of the vowels in Spanish has a uniform pronunciation. Spanish **a** has one pronunciation, rather than the numerous pronunciations we find in English, such as in 'cake', 'art' and 'all'. Vowels are pronounced clearly, even in unstressed positions or at the end of a word.

a   as the 'u' in 'nut'
e   as the 'e' in 'met'
i   somewhere between the 'i' in 'marine' and the 'i' in 'flip'
o   as the 'o' in 'hot'
u   after g and followed by e or i, this letter is silent;
    elsewhere, as the 'oo' in 'too';
    when written with diaeresis (ü), as the 'w' in 'watch'

CONSONANTS

Some Spanish consonants are pronounced the same as their English counterparts. Pronunciation of other consonants varies according to the vowel it precedes. The Spanish alphabet also contains three consonants which aren't found in the English alphabet: ch, ll and ñ.

b   somewhere between English 'b' and 'v'. Try saying this with your lips slightly closed, (the English 'b' is pronounced with closed lips) and your top teeth on your bottom lip (the English 'v' is pronounced this way, though with open lips).
    As as the 'b' in 'book' at the start of a word or after m, n or ñ.
c   when followed by a, o, u or a consonant, as the 'c' in 'cat'; before e or i, as the 's' in 'sin'

PRONUNCIATION

ch	as the 'ch' in 'choose'
d	at the start of a word, as the 'd' in 'dog'; elsewhere as the 'th' in 'then'
g	before e or i, similar to the 'h' in 'hit'; at the start of a word, as the 'g' in 'gate' before a, o and u
h	always silent
j	as the 'h' in 'haste'
ll	between the 'ly' sound in 'million' and the 'y' in 'yes'
ñ	as the 'ny' in 'canyon'
q	as the 'k' in 'kiss'
r	a rolled 'r' sound; a longer and stronger sound at the start of a word or when written as double 'rr'
s	as the 's' in 'sin'; often not pronounced at the end of a word.
v	the same sound as 'b' (Spanish)
x	between two vowels, as the 'x' in 'taxi'; before a consonant, as the 's' in 'sin'
z	as the 's' in 'sin'

Semiconsonant

y	at the end of a word or when it stands alone, as the 'i' in 'marine'; as a consonant, between the 'y' in 'yellow' and the 'g' in 'beige'

STRESS

There are three general rules regarding stress:

- For words ending in 'n', 's' or a vowel, stress is placed on the second-last syllable.

  friend   **amigo**   shoes   **zapatos**

- In words ending in a consonant other than 'n' or 's', the stress is on the final syllable.

  love   **amor**   city   **ciudad**

- Any deviation from these rules is indicated by an accent:

  here   **aquí**   tree   **árbol**
  station   **estación**   camera   **cámara**

GRAMMAR

This chapter is designed to give you an idea of how Spanish phrases are put together, providing you with the basic rules to help you to construct your own sentences.

WORD ORDER
Generally, the word order of sentences is similar to the English word order of subject-verb-object.

Ana drinks beer.   Ana bebe cerveza.

ARTICLES
In Spanish there are two articles – the definite article 'the' and the indefinite article 'a'. Spanish has feminine and masculine forms as well as singular and plural forms for each.

Feminine

| the house | la casa | the houses | las casas |
| a house | una casa | some houses | unas casas |

Masculine

| the book | el libro | the books | los libros |
| a book | un libro | some books | unos libros |

NOUNS
Nouns always have either a feminine or masculine form. Although there are some rules to help tell which nouns are masculine and which are feminine, as with all rules, there are always exceptions.

Feminine
• Nouns descriptive of females.

| the woman | la mujer |
| the girl | la chica |

- Generally, nouns ending in -a.

| the house | la casa |

- Nouns ending in -ción, -sión and -dad.

| the song | la canción |
| the university | la universidad |

Masculine
- Nouns descriptive of men.

| the man | el hombre |
| the boy | el chico |

- Generally, nouns ending in -o and -or.

| the book | el libro |
| the engine | el motor |

- Days of the week, months, rivers, mountains, seas and oceans.

| Monday | el lunes |
| the Mediterranean | el Mediterráneo |

Plurals
In general, you can simply add -s to a noun to form the plural.

| bed | cama | beds | camas |

If a noun ends in a consonant, make the plural by adding -es.

| flower | flor | flowers | flores |

Diminutives
The use of diminutive suffixes is common in Costa Rica. These are endings to nouns and adjectives to express smallness or affection, such as when expressing the smallness and cuteness of a puppy. Common diminutive suffixes are -ita/o, -cita/o, as well as -illa/o and -cilla/o.

café	coffee	cafecito
amor	love	amorcito
animal	animal	animalito
perro	dog	perrito

PRONOUNS
Subject Pronouns

The English singular 'you' has three forms in Spanish – **tú** and **vos**, which are generally used in familiar and informal situations, and **usted**, which is a more formal term but is still frequently used in Costa Rica. It's best to play it safe and address new acquaintances using **usted**. Unlike in many other Spanish-speaking countries, even children are sometimes addressed using **usted**. As a general rule, you should respond in the same form that you're addressed in.

In Costa Rica, the term **vosotras/os**, the plural form of 'you', has completely disappeared, and **ustedes** is now commonly used in both formal and informal situations.

I	yo	we	nosotras/os
you	tú/vos* (inf)		
you	usted (pol)	you	ustedes (pl, pol)
she/it	ella	they	ellas/ellos
he/it	él		

*vos is much less common than tú

GRAMMAR

You'll find that the subject pronoun is usually omitted in Spanish, because the subject is understood from the verb ending.

I'm travelling to Europe.　　**Viajo a Europa.**
　　　　　　　　　　　　　(lit: I-travel to Europe)

However, if there's a chance of ambiguity, the subject pronoun should be included.

Object Pronouns

Direct object pronouns are used in Spanish to refer to people as 'him', 'them', and so on.

me	me	him/it; you (m, pol)	lo
you (inf)	te	us	nos
her/it; you (f, pol)	la	you/them	las/los

I don't know him.   **No lo conozco.**
                         (lit: not him I-know)

Indirect object pronouns are used to describe relations such as 'to him' and 'to them'.

| to me | me | to her/him; to you (pol) | le |
| to you (inf) | te | to you/them | les |

I'm talking to her.   **Le hablo.**
                         (lit: to-her I-speak)

VERBS

There are three different categories of verbs in Spanish – those ending in -ar, -er and -ir. Tenses are formed by adding endings to the verb stem, and these endings vary according to whether the verb is an -ar, -er or -ir verb. Although there are quite a few exceptions to the rules when forming these endings, the following standard forms are useful to know:

	-ar	-er	-ir
Infinitive	comprar	comer	vivir
	(to buy)	(to eat)	(to live)
Stem	compr-	com-	viv-

As the informal plural form of 'you', **vosotras/os**, is never used in Costa Rica, it hasn't been included in the following tables, and remember that the polite form of singular 'you' is more common than the informal.

Present Tense

	-ar	-er	-ir
I	compro	como	vivo
you (inf)	compras	comes	vives
she/he/it/you (pol)	compra	come	vive
we	compramos	comemos	vivimos
you/they	compran	comen	viven

Future Tense

This is the easiest tense to form as the endings are the same regardless of whether the verb ends with -ar, -er or -ir. You simply add the endings to the infinitive of the verb:

	-ar	-er	-ir
I	compraré	comeré	viviré
you (inf)	comprarás	comerás	vivirás
she/he/it; you (pol)	comprará	comerá	vivirá
we	compraremos	comeremos	viviremos
you/they	comprarán	comerán	vivirán

Going to ...

A more common way of creating the future tense, particularly when you're discussing the immediate future, is to use the verb ir, 'to go', in the present tense, followed by the preposition a, 'to/at', plus the infinitive form of the verb.

I	am going to ...	voy a ...
you (inf)	are going to ...	vas a...
he/she/it; you (pol)	is/are going to ...	va a...
we	are going to ...	vamos a...
you/they	are going to ...	van a...

I'm going to eat later. **Voy a comer más tarde.**
(lit: I-go to to-eat more late)

GRAMMAR

Past Tense

There are three ways of referring to the past:

1) The **preterite**, or simple past tense, is used to express completed past actions, which usually only happened once.

	-ar	-er	-ir
I	compré	comí	viví
you (inf)	compraste	comiste	viviste
he/she/it; you (pol)	compró	comió	vivió
we	compramos	comimos	vivimos
you/they	compraron	comieron	vivieron

I bought a shirt yesterday.   **Compré una camisa ayer.**
(lit: I-bought a shirt yesterday)

2) The **imperfect** is used for past actions which went on for some time, happened repeatedly, or were going on when a completed action (simple past) took place. So, in the sentence 'I was reading when John knocked at the door', 'I was reading' is the imperfect as it was going on during the time that 'John knocked'. The imperfect is expressed in English as 'I was buying', 'I bought' (on several occasions) or 'I used to buy'.

	-ar	-er	-ir
I	compraba	comía	vivía
you (inf)	comprabas	comías	vivías
he/she/it; you (pol)	compraba	comía	vivía
we	comprábamos	comíamos	vivíamos
you/they	compraban	comían	vivían

We were living together
in Scotland.   **Vivíamos juntos en Escocia.**
(lit: we-were-living together in
Scotland)

They ate all day.   **Comían todo el día.**
(lit: they-ate all the day)

GRAMMAR

3) The **present perfect** is used for a completed past action which implies a strong connection with the present. It's formed with the verb **haber**, 'to have', plus the past participle.

An example of the present perfect in English is 'I have bought' – the verb 'have' plus the past participle of 'to buy'. Generally, to create the past participle for -**ar** verbs, you add -**ado** to the stem. For -**er** and -**ir** verbs, the past participle is the stem plus -**ido**.

comprar	to buy	becomes	**comprado**	bought
comer	to eat	becomes	**comido**	ate
vivir	to live	becomes	**vivido**	lived

The Subjunctive Tense

The subjunctive is frequently used in Spanish, unlike English, and is therefore often ignored or misused. The subjunctive form is used to denote irreality, doubt or desire.

	-ar	-er	-ir
I	compre	coma	viva
you (inf)	compres	comas	vivas
she/he/it; you (pol)	compre	coma	viva
we	compremos	comamos	vivamos
you/they	compren	coman	vivan

I don't want that to happen.	No quiero que suceda esto.
I hope he comes.	Espero que venga.
I doubt we'll eat early tonight.	Dudo que cenemos pronto esta noche.

The Gerund

The gerund is the verb which, in English, is expressed by the addition of '-ing' to the verb stem. In Spanish, the equivalent is -**ando** for -**ar** verbs, and -**endo** for both -**er** and -**ir** verbs, and they're used after the verb estar.

It's raining.	**Está lloviendo.** (lit: it-is raining)

However, in Spanish, it's often common to simply use the present tense for the same meaning. Thus 'It's raining' can also be **llueve**. 'We're going' is usually just **Vamos**; 'I'm going' is **Voy**.

TO KNOW

In Spanish, there are two words which mean 'to know'. One is **saber**, 'to have knowledge of, be aware of, be able to', and the other is **conocer**, 'to be acquainted with a person or place'.

Have you heard the latest?	¿Sabes lo último?
	(lit: you-know it latest?)
Do you know my brother?	¿Conoces a* mi hermano?
	(lit: you-know a my brother?)

* when used with animate beings the preposition **a** always follows the verb

TO HAVE

The verb 'to have' has two forms in Spanish – **haber** and **tener**

Haber

The verb **haber** is used as an auxiliary verb to form the present perfect tense, as in 'I have seen'.

Haber			
I have	he	we have	hemos
you (inf) have	has	you/they have	han
she/he/it has; you (pol) have	ha		

We've bought tickets.	**Hemos comprado billetes.**
	(lit: we-have bought tickets)

For the past participles of other verbs, see page 24.

GRAMMAR

Hay

One word you'll often hear in Costa Rica is the impersonal form of haber, which is hay. This is used to mean 'there is/are', as well as in questions meaning 'are/is there?' or 'do you have ...'.

Do you have any rooms?	¿Hay habitaciones?
	(lit: there-are rooms?)
There isn't/aren't any.	No (no) hay.
	(lit: no (not) there-is/are)

KEY VERBS

to arrive	llegar
to be	ser/estar
to bring	traer
to come	venir
to cost	costar/valer
to depart (leave)	partir; salir de
to do	hacer
to go	ir/partir
to have	tener/haber
to know (someone)	conocer
to know (something)	saber
to like	gustarle/apreciar
to live (life)	vivir
to live (somewhere)	vivir/ocupar
to make	hacer/fabricar
to meet	encontrar/conocer
to need	necesitar
to prefer	preferir
to return	volver/regresar
to say	decir
to stay (remain)	quedarse
to stay (somewhere)	alojarse/hospedarse
to take	llevar
to understand	entender/omprender
to want	querer/desear

GRAMMAR

Tener

This form of 'to have' can be used to express both possession and compulsion (having to do something – see page 26).

Tener			
I have	tengo	we have	tenemos
you (inf) have	tienes	you/they have	tienen
she/he/it/has; you (pol) have	tiene		

A small number of phrases with the construction 'to be + adjective' in English, are expressed in Spanish by tener 'to have' + noun (see also estar, page 23).

to be hungry	tener hambre	(lit: to-have hunger)
to be thirsty	tener sed	(lit: to-have thirst)
to be afraid	tener miedo	(lit: to-have fear)
to be right (correct)	tener razón	(lit: to-have reason)

TO BE

The verb 'to be' has two forms in Spanish – ser and estar. To know exactly when to use which verb takes practice, but here are some basic rules.

Ser

Ser			
I am	soy	we are	somos
you (inf) are	eres/sos*	you/they are	son
she/he/it is; you (pol) are	es		
* Sos is less common			

The verb ser is used in situations that have a degree of permanence about them.

- characteristics of persons or things

  The book is yellow.   **El libro es amarillo.**
                                 (lit: the book is yellow)

- occupations and nationality

  I'm a student.   **Soy estudiante.**
                                 (I-am student)

- telling the time and location of events

  It's one o'clock.   **Es la una.**
                                 (lit: it-is the one)

Estar

Estar			
I am	estoy	we are	estamos
you (inf) are	estás	you/they are	están
she/he/it is; you (pol) are	está		

The verb estar implies a characteristic which is temporary, or which is the result of an action.

  The food is cold.   **La comida está fría.**
                                 (lit: the food it-is cold)

- it's used with the location of persons or things

  I'm in Quepos.   **Estoy en Quepos.**
                                 (lit: I-am in Quepos)

- it is used to indicate mood

  They are happy.   **Están contentos.**
                                 (lit: they-are happy)

GRAMMAR

KEY VERBS

Regular Verbs

The following verb forms are regular forms. Most other verbs follow the same conjugations. The three forms are those ending in -ar, -er and -ir.

As the informal plural form of 'you', vosotros is never used in Costa Rica, it hasn't been included in the following tables, and remember that the polite form of singular 'you' is more common than the informal.

comer (to eat)	present	simple past	imperfect	future
	past participle: (haber) comido			
I	como	comí	comía	comeré
you (inf)	comes	comiste	comías	comerás
he/she/it; you (pol)	come	comió	comía	comerá
we	comemos	comimos	comíamos	comeremos
you/they	comen	comieron	comían	comerán

vivir (to live)	present	simple past	imperfect	future
	past participle: (haber) vivido			
I	vivo	viví	vivía	viviré
you (inf)	vives	viviste	vivías	vivirás
he/she/it; you (pol)	vive	vivió	vivía	vivirá
we	vivimos	vivimos	vivíamos	viviremos
you/they	viven	vivieron	vivían	vivirán

Irregular Verbs

estar (to be)	present	simple past	imperfect	future
	past participle: (haber) estado			
I	estoy	estuve	estaba	estaré
you (inf)	estás	estuviste	estabas	estarás
he/she/it; you (pol)	está	estuvo	estaba	estará
we	estamos	estuvimos	estábamos	estaremos
you/they	están	estuvieron	estaban	estarán

ir (to go)	present	simple past	imperfect	future
	past participle: (haber) ido			
I	voy	fui	iba	iré
you (inf)	vas	fuiste	ibas	irás
he/she/it; you (pol)	va	fue	iba	irá
we	vamos	fuimos	íbamos	iremos
you/they	van	fueron	iban	irán

GRAMMAR

haber (to have)

past participle: (haber) habido

	present	simple past	imperfect	future
I	he	hube	había	habré
you (inf)	has	hubiste	habías	habrás
he/she/it; you (pol)	ha	hubo	había	habrá
we	hemos	hubimos	habíamos	habremos
you/they	han	hubieron	habían	habrán

ser (to be)

past participle: (haber) sido

	present	simple past	imperfect	future
I	soy	fui	era	seré
you (inf)	eres	fuiste	eras	serás
he/she/it; you (pol)	es	fue	era	será
we	somos	fuimos	éramos	seremos
you/they	son	fueron	eran	serán

tener (to have)

past participle: (haber) tenido

	present	simple past	imperfect	future
I	tengo	tuve	tenía	tendré
you (inf)	tienes	tuviste	tenías	tendrás
he/she/it; you (pol)	tiene	tuvo	tenía	tendrá
we	tenemos	tuvimos	teníamos	tendremos
you/they	tienen	tuvieron	tenían	tendrán

hacer (to make/do)

past participle: (haber) hecho

	present	simple past	imperfect	future
I	hago	hice	hacía	haré
you (inf)	haces	hiciste	hacías	harás
he/she/it; you (pol)	hace	hizo	hacía	hará
we	hacemos	hicimos	hacíamos	haremos
you/they	hacen	hicieron	hacían	harán

querer (to want)

past participle: (haber) querido

	present	simple past	imperfect	future
I	quiero	quise	quería	querré
you (inf)	quieres	quisiste	querías	querrás
he/she/it; you (pol)	quiere	quiso	quería	querrá
we	queremos	quisimos	queríamos	querremos
you/they	quieren	quisieron	querían	querrán

GRAMMAR

MODALS
Must/Have To/Need To
In order to express having to do something, you can use the verb **tener** followed by **que** and then the infinitive of the verb.

I have to change some money.	**Tengo que cambiar dinero.**

Can/To Be Able
There are several ways to express 'can' and 'to be able'. The verb **poder** can be used, while you might also hear **es posible (que)**, 'it's possible (that)'.

Can you do it?	**¿Puedes hacerlo?;**
	¿Es posible hacerlo?

To Like
In Spanish, when expressing that you like something, you literally say that 'something pleases you'. The verb **gustar**, 'to please/taste', is used with an indirect object pronoun (see page 16).

I like beer.	**Me gusta la cerveza.**
	(lit: me it-pleases the beer)
We like it.	**Nos gusta.**
	(lit: us it-pleases)

ADJECTIVES
Adjectives in Spanish agree in gender and number with the nouns they describe, so they have different endings depending on whether the noun is masculine, feminine, singular or plural. Unlike English, they almost always come after the noun.

a white hat	**un sombrero blanco**
some white hats	**unos sombreros blancos**

Adjectives of quantity - such as 'much', 'a lot of', 'little/few', 'too much' – cardinal and ordinal numbers, and possessive adjectives always precede the noun.

GRAMMAR

a lot of tourists	muchos turistas
first class	primera clase
my car	mi carro/auto

Comparatives

more ... than	easier than	más fácil que
más ... que	less easy than	menos fácil que
less ... than	as easy as	tan fácil como
menos ...que	as beautiful as	tan bonito como
as ... as	better	mejor
tan ... como	worse	peor

Superlatives

the most ...	the easiest	el más fácil
el más ...	the least easy	el menos fácil
the least ...	the best	el mejor
el menos ...	the worst	el peor

POSSESSION

Possession can be indicated in several ways. The most common way is by using possessive adjectives which agree in number and gender with the noun they describe. They're always placed before the noun.

Possessive Adjectives

	singular	plural
my	mi	mis
your (inf)	tu	tus
his/her/its; your (pol)	su	sus
our	nuestra/o	nuestras/os
your/their	su	sus

GRAMMAR

my country	mi país
your (inf) hands	tus manos

Another way to indicate possession is by using possessive pronouns, which also agree in number and gender with the noun and are placed after it.

Possessive Pronouns

	singular	plural
mine	mía/o	mías/os
yours (inf)	tuya/o	tuyas/os
hers/his/its; yours (pol)	suya/o	suyas/os
ours	nuestra/o	nuestras/os
yours/theirs	suya/o	suyas/os

The house is mine.	La casa es mía.
These passports are ours.	Estos pasaportes son nuestros.

QUESTIONS

All questions in Spanish involve a rise in intonation at the end of a sentence. In written Spanish, a question is introduced by an inverted question mark – this is a clear indication to change your intonation.

You're (pl) leaving early tomorrow?	¿Se van mañana temprano? (lit: you you-go tomorrow early?)

Question Words

Where?	¿Dónde?	What?	¿Qué?
Why?	¿Por qué?	How?	¿Cómo?
When?	¿Cuándo?		
Who? (sg)/(pl)		¿Quién?/¿Quiénes?	
Which?/What? (sg)		¿Cuál?	
Which?/What? (pl)		¿Cuáles?	

GRAMMAR

NEGATIVES

To form the negative in a sentence, place **no** before the verb.

I don't know what
the time is.

No sé qué hora es.

Contrary to English, you can use double negatives in Spanish.

I don't have anything.

No tengo nada.
(lit: no I-have nothing)

MISTAKES TO WATCH FOR
– ENGLISH SPEAKERS

It's useful to know what the most common mistakes are for English speakers. By checking this list from time to time, you can remind yourself of possible mistakes to avoid.

* In English, adjectives are placed before the noun (the big dog), so it's easy to forget that Spanish generally places them after the noun.

  el perro bravo ✓   not   el bravo perro ✗
  la casa blanca ✓   not   la blanca casa ✗

* The existence of two verbs in Spanish for the English 'to be' is a real headache for English-speakers, who frequently confuse them. Follow the basic rules outlined in the Grammar section, page 22.

  Ella es joven.   ✓   not   Ella está joven.   ✗
  Isabel está en San Jose. ✓   not   Isabel es en San Jose. ✗

* In Spanish, to say you like something, you say 'something is pleasing to you', using the verb gustar ('to please/taste') and the pronouns me, te, le, os, nos, les to indicate who it is pleasing to (see page 26).

GRAMMAR

> Me gusta Costa Rica.   ✓   not   Me gusto Costa Rica.   ✗
> Nos gustan las patatas. ✓   not   Nos gustamos las
>   patatas.   ✗

- The subjunctive is frequently used in Spanish, unlike English, and is therefore often ignored or misused. You won't be misunderstood if you don't use the subjunctive, but it does help to get it right. See page 19 for more details.

> Quiero que venga   not   Quiero que viene
>   conmigo al cine. ✓   al cine.   ✗

- In English, there's only one verb for 'to know', while Spanish has saber, 'to have knowledge of, be aware of, be able to do something', as well as conocer, 'to be acquainted with people and places'. See page 20 for more details.

> ¿Conoce a mi hermano? ✓ not   ¿Sabe a mi hermano? ✗
> ¿Saben leer?   ✓ not   ¿Conocen leer?   ✗

GRAMMAR

ENCUENTROS

MEETING PEOPLE

YOU SHOULD KNOW   DEBE SABER ...

If you don't remember any other Spanish words, these will be the ones that will stay in your mind – the essential greetings and civilities that exist in any language.

Hello.	¡Hola!
Hi. (in passing)	¿Adiós?
Goodbye.	¡Adiós!
Yes/No.	Sí/No.
Excuse me.	Perdón.
Please.	Por favor.
Thank you.	Gracias.
Many thanks.	Muchas gracias.
May I?; Do you mind?	¿Puedo?; ¿Me permite?
Sorry. (excuse me)	Lo siento; Discúlpeme.
That's fine. You're welcome.	De nada. (Con) mucho gusto.

THEY MAY SAY

You may hear people saying that they're **nerviosa/o**. This doesn't always translate directly as 'nervous' but more often as what we may call 'nervy'.

   (Tener) vergüenza translated directly into English means '(to have) shame', but simply means to be embarrassed or shy. **Vergüenza** is actually more subtle than **avergonzado** which has the emphasized meaning that you are frequently embarrassed or a shy person habitually.

GREETINGS   SALUDOS

In more traditional rural areas, where machismo is strong, men greet each other by shaking hands, and often do little more than nod to women. Women often shake hands in more urban areas, and in San José, friends may be greeted with a light kiss on the cheek. It's acceptable for men to hug women they know relatively well.

Good morning.	Buenos días; ¿Como amaneció? (lit: how you-woke-up?)
Good afternoon. (until about 8pm)	Buenas tardes.
Good evening/night.	Buenas noches.
Hello. (said in passing)	¿Adios?
How are you? (inf/pol)	¿Qué tal?; ¿Cómo está usted?
Well, thanks.	Bien, gracias; Bien, bien.
Not too bad.	Más o menos.
Not so good.	Pues, no muy bien.
See you later.	Hasta luego.
See you tomorrow.	Hasta mañana.
Bye.	Adiós.

¡HOLA!

FORMS OF ADDRESS
FORMAS DE SALUDOS

Mrs	Señora/Doña
Mr	Señor/Don
Miss	Señorita

It's become a lot less common for women to be addressed as **señorita**. It's more common now to use **señora** for all women, regardless of age or marital status. However, some 'señoritas' (unmarried women) may take offence when addressed as 'señora'.

companion	compañera/o; compa (col)
friend	amiga/o
mate	ma'e/loco/viejo/compa/ hermano

FIRST ENCOUNTERS
PRIMEROS ENCUENTROS

What's your name? (inf/pol)	¿Cómo te llamas?; ¿Cómo se llama usted?
My name's ...	Me llamo ...; Soy...; Me dicen ... (inf)
I'm a friend of (Maria).	Soy amiga/o de (María).
I'd like to introduce you to ...	Quisiera presentarle a ...
His/Her name is ...	Se llama ...
I'm pleased to meet you.	Mucho gusto; Encantada/o de conocerle.

HEY, YOU

Although **usted** is the formal manner to address another person, it's widely used in Costa Rica. Whereas in many Spanish speaking countries **usted** is only used when speaking to those in a senior position, such as parents, teachers and bosses, even young children are addressed using **usted** in Costa Rica.

It's a good idea to always use **usted** in any friendly situation, unless specifically asked to use **tú**.

MEETING PEOPLE

I'm here (on) ...	Estoy aquí ...
holiday	de vacaciones
business	en viaje de negocios
studying	estudiando

How long have you been here?	¿Cuánto tiempo lleva aquí?
Where are you staying?	¿Dónde se queda?
I've been here (three days).	Llevo aquí (tres días).
How long are you here for?	¿Cuánto tiempo te vas a quedar?

We're here for (two weeks).	Nos quedaremos (dos)
I like (Tamarindo) very much.	Me encanta (Tamarindo).
Are you on your own?	¿Vines sola/o?
I'm with my partner.	He venido con mi compañera/o.

It was nice talking to you.	Me encanto hablar con usted.
I have to get going now.	Ahora tengo que irme; Tengo que largarme. (col)

I had a great day/evening.	La pase muy bien.
Hope to see you again soon.	Espero verle pronto.
We must do this again	¡Tenemos que hacerlo de nuevo!

I'll give you a call.	Le llamaré.
See you soon.	Le veo pronto; Nos vemos pronto.

DID YOU KNOW ... The word **gringo**, used by Costa Ricans to refer to a person from an English-speaking country, supposedly originated in the conflict between Mexican and American soldiers on the border between the two countries. It comes directly from English, 'green go!', green referring to the colour of the military uniforms.

MEETING PEOPLE

NATIONALITIES   NACIONALIDADES

Unfortunately, we can't list all countries here, however you'll find that many country names in Spanish are similar to English. Remember though that even if a word looks like the English equivalent, it will have a Spanish pronunciation. For instance, Japan is pronounced *hah-pon*. Listed here are some country names that differ more considerably.

Where are you from?	¿De dónde es?
Are you from around here?	¿Es de por aquí?

I'm from ...	Soy de ...
Canada	Canadá
England	Inglaterra
Germany	Alemania
Holland; The Netherlands	Holanda; los Paises Bajos
New Zealand	Nueva Zelanda
Scotland	Escocia
Scandinavia	Escandinavia
Switzerland	Suiza
the USA	los Estados Unidos
Have you ever been to my country?	¿Ha estado en mi país?
What's your home town/ region like?	¿Cómo es su ciudad/región?

MEETING PEOPLE

I come from a/the ...	Vengo de ...; Soy de ...
I live in a/the ...	Vivo en ...
city	la ciudad
countryside	el campo
mountains	las montañas
seaside	la costa
suburbs of ...	a las afueras de ...
village	un pueblo

CULTURAL DIFFERENCES

DIFERENCIAS CULTURALES

How do you do this in your country?	¿Cómo se hace esto en su país?
Is this a local or national custom?	¿Es esta una costumbre local o nacional?
I don't want to offend you (sg/pl).	No quiero ofenderlo/ofenderlos.
I'm sorry, it's not the custom in my country.	Lo siento, pero esto no es una costumbre en mi país.
I don't mind watching, but I'd prefer not to participate.	No me importa observar, pero prefiero no participar.
In my country we ...	En mi país ...
My culture/religion doesn't allow me to ...	Mi cultura/religión no me permite ...
practise this	estas prácticas
eat/drink this	esta comida/bebida

AGE

EDAD

How old are you (inf)?	¿Cuántos años tienes?
I'm ... years old.	Tengo ... años.
You (inf) don't look it!	¡No te pareces!

(See Numbers, page 179 for your particular age.)

MEETING PEOPLE

OCCUPATIONS

Where do you (inf) work?
What's your (pol) profession?

I'm a/an ...
artist
businesswoman/man
doctor
driver
engineer
factory worker
homemaker
journalist
lawyer
mechanic
musician
nurse
office worker
priest
scientist
secretary
self-employed
student
teacher
waiter
writer

EMPLEO

¿En qué trabajas?
¿Cuál es su profesión?

Soy ...
artista
mujer/hombre de negocios
doctor/a; médico
chofer
ingeniera/o
obrera/o
ama de casa
periodista
abogada/o
mecánica/o
música/o
enfermera/o
oficinista; empleada/o
sacerdote/padre
científica/o
secretaria/o
trabajador(a) independiente
estudiante
profesor(a)
mesera/o
escritor(a)

UPE

Instead of knocking on the door of a house, calling out upe (pronounced *oo-pay*) has a similar meaning to 'Hello, is anyone there?' In more rural areas, it's not uncommon for front doors to be open, and it's rude to simply walk into someone's house without announcing your arrival.

MEETING PEOPLE

I'm ...	Estoy ...
retired	pensionado
unemployed	sin empleo; desempleada/o
Do you enjoy your work?	¿Le gusta su trabajo?
How long have you been in your job?	¿Cuánto tiempo tiene en su trabajo?
What are you studying?	¿Qué estudia?
I'm studying ...	Estudio ...
art	arte
business	negocios
education	educación
engineering	ingeniería
humanities	humanidades
languages	idiomas
law	derecho
medicine	medicina
science	ciencias
social sciences	ciencias sociales
Spanish	español

COSTARRICENSES

The correct name for Costa Rican people is Costarricense(s). This word is tricky – notice the double 'r' needs to be trilled, and that it's Costarricences not Costarricances (as in Costa Rica).

RELIGION   RELIGIÓN

Costa Rica is predominantly Catholic, although there's a growing number of Protestants and Evangelicals. Religion seems to be more of a personal and private matter than the omnipresent Catholicism of other Latin American countries. Most African-Costa Ricans (see page 159, Limón Creole) are Protestant, with a contingent of Rastafarians.

What's your religion?	¿Cuál es su religión?
I'm ...	Soy ...
Buddhist	budista
Catholic	católica/o
Christian	cristiana/o
Hindu	hindú
Jewish	judía/o
Muslim	musulmana/musulmán

I'm Catholic, but not practicing.	Soy católica/o pero no voy a la iglesia.
I think I believe in God, or something like God.	Tal vez creo en Dios, o en algo similar.
I believe in destiny/fate.	Creo en el destino.
I'm not religious.	No soy religiosa/o.
I'm agnostic.	Soy agnóstica/o.
I'm an atheist.	Soy atea/o.

FEELINGS

SENTIMIENTOS

I'm ...	Tengo ...
Are you ...?	¿Tiene ...?
afraid	miedo
cold	frío
hot	calor
hungry	hambre
in a hurry	prisa

keen to ...	ganas de ...
right	razón
sleepy	sueño
thirsty	sed

TICOS

Costa Ricans are often referred to as Ticos. This nickname stems from the Costa Rican people's affinity for putting 'cutesy' -(t)itao and -(t)icao suffixes at the ends of words to add emphasis. Something that's very small isn't just muy chico, it's chiquitico or even chiquitiquiticao.

MEETING PEOPLE

I'm ...	Estoy ...		
Are you ...?	¿Está ...?		
angry	enojada/o	tired	cansada/o
happy	feliz	well	bien
sad	triste	worried	preocupada/o

I'm very sorry. (condolence)	Lo siento mucho.
I'm grateful.	Le agradezco mucho.

BREAKING THE LANGUAGE BARRIER
ROMPIENDO LAS DIFERENCIAS DE IDIOMA

Do you speak English?	¿Habla usted inglés?
Does anyone speak English?	¿Hay alguien que hable inglés?
I don't speak Spanish.	No hablo español.
I speak a little Spanish.	Hablo un poco de español.
I'm learning.	Estoy aprendiendo.
Excuse my Spanish!	¡Perdona mi español!
I (don't) understand.	(No) entiendo.
Do you understand?	¿Me entiende?
Could you speak more slowly please?	Más despacio, por favor.
Could you repeat that?	¿Puede repetirlo?
Could you write that down please?	¿Puede escribirlo, por favor?
How do you say ...?	¿Cómo se dice ...?
What's this called in Spanish?	¿Cómo se dice esto en español?
What does ... mean?	¿Qué significa ...?
How do you pronounce this word?	¿Cómo se pronuncia esta palabra?
Pardon?/What?	¿Cómo?

MANERAS DE VIAJAR

GETTING AROUND

Bus is the most common form of transport in Costa Rica, although you may find yourself travelling on anything from donkeys to scooters or pick up trucks. Taxis are also common in larger towns, including four-wheel drive taxis for travellers with higher budgets.

FINDING YOUR WAY

Excuse me, can you help me please?

How do I get to the ...?
Where's the ...?
    bus station
    bus stop
    city centre
    port
    taxi stand
    ticket office

Is it far from/near here?
Where are we now?
What's the best way to get there?
Can I walk there?
Can you show me (on the map)?
Is there another way to get there?

BUSCANDO EL CAMINO

¿Perdón, puede usted ayudarme por favor?

¿Cómo se va a ...?
¿Dónde está ...?
    la estación de autobuses
    la parada de autobús
    el centro de la ciudad
    el puerto
    la parada de taxis
    la ticketería; la boletería

¿Está lejos/cerca de aquí?
¿Dónde estamos ahora?
¿Cómo se puede ir?

¿Se puede ir andando?
¿Me lo puede mostrar (en el mapa)?
¿Hay otra manera de ir allá?

GETTING AROUND

DIRECTIONS   PREGUNTANDO DIRECCIONES

Most people are willing to help when you ask directions, however, in their efforts to be helpful, some people won't admit to not knowing a direction and might misdirect you. A good trick is to never point in an assumed direction and ask 'yes' or 'no' if that direction is correct. Always let the person you've asked signal the direction and judge from the speed of their response and their apparent level of confidence whether they know what they're talking about or not.

Turn left ...	Doble a la izquierda ...
Turn right ...	Doble a la derecha ...
Cross the road ...	Cruce la calle ...
at the next corner	en la próxima esquina
at the traffic lights	en la parada
at the roundabout	en la rotonda
Go straight ahead.	Siga derecho/directo.
Straight ahead.	Adelante.
It's (two) ... down.	Está a (dos) ... de aquí.
streets	calles
blocks	cientos metros
	(lit: hundred meters)

UP THE CREEK

Distance in Costa Rica is often measured in lengths of around 100 meters, as most blocks are said to be about that length. If someone tells you that the post office is 700 meters to the left, don't start counting your paces, just go about seven blocks.

Directions will often be explained in terms of landmarks, as well as a few major streets. In rural areas, directions may be given in relation to natural landmarks like streams or prominent trees.

after	después de	in front of	enfrente/delante de
behind	detrás de	near	cerca
between	entre	next to	al lado de
far	lejos	opposite	enfrente de
uphill	para arriba	downhill	para abajo

| avenue | avenida | square | plaza |
| boulevard | bulevar | street | calle/paseo |

| north | norte | east | este |
| south | sur | west | oeste |

ADDRESSES   DIRECCIONES

Costa Ricans almost always explain addresses in terms of land-marks and, although numbered addresses exist in places such as San José and other larger Costa Rican cities, many people may be unfamiliar with them. Most addresses also have the province and closest large town/city indicated. In rural areas, addresses may include landmarks like trees, streams or other natural features. A house address may read something like:

> Ana Fernández
> 2km despues de la fabrica hacia el Aguila
> (2km after the coffee factory on the way to el Aguila)
> Pejibaye de Perez Zeledon
> San Isidro el General (closest major town)
> Costa Rica
> Centroamérica

GETTING AROUND

BUYING TICKETS

Excuse me, where's the ticket office?

Where can I buy a ...?

    plane ticket
    bus/general ticket
    ticket (entertainment)

Do you have a timetable?
I want to go to ...
How much is the fare to ...?

How long does the trip take?
Is it a direct trip?
Is it full?
Do I need to book?
I'd like to book a seat to ...?

I'd like (a) ...
    one-way ticket
    return ticket
    two tickets

a/an ... fare
    adult
    child's
    pensioner
    student

first class
second class
economy class

(No) smoking, please.

COMPRANDO TICKETES

¿Disculpe, dónde está la boletería/ticketería?

¿Dónde puedo comprar un(a) ...?
    boleto
    tickete/pasaje
    entrada

¿Tiene un horario?
Quiero ir a ...
¿Cuánto vale el pasaje/ boleto/tickete a ...?

¿Cuánto se demora en llegar?
¿Es un viaje directo?
¿Está lleno?
¿Tengo que hacer reserva?
Quisiera reservar un pasaje a ...

Quisiera ...
    un boleto de ida
    un boleto de ida y vuelta
    dos boletos

una tarifa de ...
    adulto
    niño
    pensionado
    estudiante

THEY MAY SAY	
Está lleno.	It's full.

primera clase
segunda clase
clase económica/turística

Quisiera un asiento de (no) fumar.

I'd like to ... my reservation.	Quisiera ... mi reservación.
cancel	cancelar
change	cambiar
confirm	confirmar

Is it completely full?	¿Está completamente lleno?
Can I go on the standby list?	¿Puede ponerme en la lista de espera?

What time does the ... leave/arrive?	¿A qué hora sale/llega la/el ...?
boat	barco
small boat	panga
bus (city/local)	autobús/bus
bus (intercity/coach)	bus
plane	avión
train	tren

AT CUSTOMS

EN LA ADUANA

I have nothing to declare.	No tengo nada que declarar.
This is all my luggage.	Este es todo mi equipaje.
Can I go through?	¿Puedo pasar?
Do I have to declare this?	¿Tengo que declarar esto?
I'd like to declare ...	Quisiera declarar ...
Can I call my ...?	¿Puedo llamar a ... de mi país?
consulate	al consulado
embassy	la embajada

¡PERMISO! – ¡DISCULPE! – ¡PERDÓN!

The expression ¡Permiso! is useful when trying to physically get past people.

To catch someone's attention, use ¡Disculpe! or ¡Perdón!

If you accidentally bump into someone, use ¡Perdón!

Lo siento, the closest equivalent of 'I'm sorry', isn't used as casually in Costa Rican Spanish as in English.

GETTING AROUND

AIR   AEROLINEA

To get around the country, it's a lot quicker, and often not too expensive, to take internal flights rather than buses.

When's the next flight to ...?	¿Cuándo sale el próximo vuelo para ...?
How long does the flight take?	¿Cuánto tiempo dura el vuelo?
Is it a nonstop flight?	¿Es un vuelo directo?
What's the flight number?	¿Cuál es el número del vuelo?
What time do I have to check in?	¿A qué hora tengo que chequear mi equipaje?
Is there a bus to the airport?	¿Hay algún autobús para el aeropuerto?
Is there a departure tax here?	¿Hay que pagar impuestos en este aeropuerto?
How long will it be delayed?	¿Cuánto tiempo más se retrasará?
I'd like to check my luggage in.	Quisiera chequear mi equipaje.
What's the charge for each excess kilo?	¿Cuánto vale cada quilo de más?
My luggage hasn't arrived.	Mis maletas no llegaron.

No tengo nada que declarar

ADUANA

aeroplane	el avión
airport tax	el impuesto del aeropuerto
arrivals	las llegadas
baggage	el equipaje
baggage claim	la reclamación de equipajes
boarding pass	la tarjeta de embarque

check-in	la chequea de equipajes
departures	las partidas/salidas
domestic flight	el vuelo nacional
flight	el vuelo
gate	la puerta
international	internacional
passport	el pasaporte
transit lounge	el tránsito

SIGNS

ADUANA	**CUSTOMS**
ARTÍCULOS SIN IMPUESTOS	**DUTY-FREE GOODS**
INMIGRACIÓN	**IMMIGRATION CONTROL**
CONTROL DE PASAPORTE/S	**PASSPORT CONTROL**
HACIA ...	**THIS WAY TO ...**
SALIDA	**WAY OUT**

BUS   AUTOBUS

Buses are used extensively by Costa Ricans and provide a good form of transport for those interested in mingling with locals and learning something of their day-to-day lives. Keep an eye on belongings on buses and in or around bus stations.

Many hotels in San José have bus schedules for major routes from the capital, otherwise times are sometimes posted at ticket windows. Buses can be very crowded, and many have assigned seats, so if you don't want to stand for eight hours, buy your ticket ahead of time.

Where's the bus stop?	¿Dónde está la parada de autobús?
How often do buses pass by?	¿Cada cuántos minutos pasa el autobús?

Which bus goes to ...?	¿Qué autobús va a ...?

What time is the ... coach/bus?
  first
  next
  last

¿A qué hora sale el ... autobús?
  primer
  próximo
  último

Do you stop at ...? | ¿Para usted en ...?
(Two) tickets, please. | (Dos) ticketes, por favor.
Could you let me know when we get to ...? | ¿Me puede decir cuando lleguemos a ...?
Is smoking allowed on this bus? | ¿Se puede fumar en este autobús?
Excuse me. | (Con) Permiso. (when moving past someone)

I want to get off! | ¡Quiero bajarme!

Does this bus go to the ...?
  beach
  city centre
  station

¿Este autobús va a ...?
  la playa
  el centro de la ciudad
  la estación

TAXI   TAXI

It's reasonably cheap to catch taxis in Costa Rica. In many cities you must fix a price before travelling, and this may involve some bargaining. Some taxis have meters, and you must be sure it's turned on and set at the minimum tariff when you set off. Piratas, 'pirates', don't have a taxi permit and use their personal car without a meter, but offer their services at a lower price. Four-wheel drive taxis are common near rural tourist destinations. These taxis are more expensive and rarely have meters.

Remember when giving instructions that 'blocks' are often described as being 100 metres, and landmarks are useful when describing where you want to go (see Addresses, page 43).

Please take me to ...	Por favor, lléveme ...
this address	a esta dirección
the airport	al aeropuerto
the city centre	al centro de la ciudad

Are you free?	¿Está libre?
Use the meter, please.	Con taximetro, por favor.
How much is it to go to ...?	¿Cuánto cuesta/vale ir a ...?
Does that include luggage?	¿Incluye esto el equipaje?
For two people?	¿Para dos personas?
It's too much!	¡Es demasiado!; ¡Es demasiadisísimo! (col)

Can you take (five) people?	¿Puede llevar (cinco) personas?

Do you have change of 500 colones?	¿Tiene cambio de quinientos colones?
Please slow down.	Vaya más despacio, por favor.
Please hurry.	Apurate, por favor.
The next corner, please.	En la próxima esquina, por favor.

Continue!	¡Siga!
The next street to the left/right.	En la próxima calle a la izquierda/derecha.
Here's fine, thank you.	Aquí está bien, gracias.
Stop here!	¡Pare aquí!
Please wait here.	Espere aquí, por favor.
How much do I owe you? (pol/inf)	¿Cuánto le debo?; ¿Cuánto es?

CHEPE

The nickname for José is Chepe, and this is also the nickname for Costa Rica's capital, San José. Rumour has it that if you ask a taxi driver to take you from the airport to Chepe instead of San José, they'll assume you know Costa Rica well and will give you a fair price.

CAR   CARRO

Although relatively expensive, renting cars, especially four-wheel drive trucks, is becoming increasingly popular. Whether you're in your own or in a rental car, this section covers the essentials.

Where can I hire a car?	¿Dónde puedo alquilar/rentar un carro?
How much is it daily/weekly?	¿Cuánto cuesta por día/ semana?
Does that include insurance/ mileage?	¿Incluye el seguro/ kilometraje?
Where's the closest petrol station?	¿Dónde queda la gasolinera/ bomba más cercana?
I want ... litres of petrol (gas).	Quiero ... litros de gasolina.
I want (2000 colones) worth of petrol.	Quiero (dos mil colones) en gasolina.
Please fill the tank.	Lléneme el tanque, por favor.

SIGNS

ACCESO PERMANENTE	24-HOUR ACCESS
ACCESO PROHIBIDO	NO ENTRY
CEDA EL PASO	GIVE WAY
CONSTRUCCIÓN DE CARRETERAS	ROADWORKS
DESVIACIÓN	DETOUR
DESVÍO	DETOUR
DISMINUYA SU VELOCIDAD	SLOWDOWN
NO PASE	DO NOT OVERTAKE
PARE	STOP
PEATONES	PEDESTRIANS
PELIGRO	DANGER
PRECAUCIÓN	CAUTION
PROHIBIDO ESTACIONAR	NO PARKING
SALIDA	EXIT
UNA VIA	ONE WAY

Please check the ...	Por favor, revise el ...
oil	nivel del aceite
water	nivel del agua
air	aire
How long can I park here?	¿Cuánto tiempo puedo estacionar aquí?
Does this road lead to ...?	¿Se va a ... por esta carretera?
air	el aire
battery	la batería/el acumulador
brakes	los frenos
car	el carro/auto
clutch	el embrague
driving licence	el permiso/la licencia de conducir
engine	el motor
garage	el taller
indicator	el indicador
lights	las luces
main road	la carretera
map	el mapa
mobile breath tester	el control de alcoholemia
motorway	la autopista
oil	el aceite
... petrol (gas)	la gasolina ...
leaded	normal
regular	con plomo
unleaded	sin plomo
petrol pump	el surtidor de gasolina
petrol station	la bomba/gasolinera
puncture	el agujero/hueco
radiator	el radiador
road map	el mapa de carreteras
seatbelt	el cinturón de seguridad

GETTING AROUND

self-service	el autoservicio
speed limit	el límite de velocidad
super	súper
tyres	la llantas (col); los neumáticos
windshield	las parabrisas

Car Problems

Problemas de carro

I need a mechanic.	Necesito un mecánico.
What make is it?	¿(De) qué marca es?
I've had a breakdown at ...	He tenido una avería en ...
The battery is dead.	La batería está descargada.
The radiator is leaking.	El radiador tiene una fuga.

I have a ... tyre.	Tengo una llanta ...
burst	estallada
flat	desinflada
punctured	ponchada

It's overheating.	Está recalentándose.
It's not working.	No funciona.
I've lost my car keys.	He perdido las llaves de mi carro.
I've run out of petrol.	Me he quedado sin gasolina.

THEY MAY SAY

De acuerdo.	OK.
Claro.	Sure.
Vámonos.	Let's go.
¡Ojo!	Careful!
Espera.	Wait.
Espera un segundo.	Just a minute.
¿Está lista/o?	Are you ready?
Estoy lista/o.	I'm ready.

BOAT   BARCO

Sometimes boat is the only form of transport available and, although they may be slow, it can be a great experience.

What time does the next ferry depart?	¿A qué hora sale el próximo barco?
Where do we get on the boat?	¿Dónde nos subimos al barco?

boat	el barco
boat (motorless)	el bote
canoe	la canoa
motorboat	la lancha/panga
pier	el embarcadero
port	el puerto
raft	la balsa
wharf	el muelle

BICYCLE   BICICLETA

Do you like cycling?	¿Le gusta andar en bicicleta?
Do you cycle?	¿Sabe andar en bicicleta?
Can you recommend a good place for a bike ride?	¿Me puede recomendar algún sitio bonito para pasear en bicicleta?
Is it within cycling distance?	¿Se puede ir en bicicleta?
Is it safe to cycle around here?	¿Es seguro andar en bicicleta aquí?
Where can I find secondhand bicycles for sale?	¿Dónde venden bicicletas de segunda mano?
Where can I hire a bicycle?	¿Dónde se alquilan bicicletas?
How much is it to hire a bicycle for the ...?	¿Cuánto vale alquilar una bicicleta por...?
hour	una hora
morning/afternoon	toda la mañana/tarde
day	todo el día

Can you lend me a padlock?	¿Me puede prestar un candado?
Can you raise/lower the seat?	¿Me puede subir/bajar el asiento?
Is it compulsory to wear a helmet?	¿Es obligatorio llevar casco?
Where can I leave the bicycle?	¿Dónde puedo dejar la bicicleta?
Can I leave the bike here?	¿Puedo dejar la bicicleta aquí?
Where are bike repairs done?	¿Dónde arreglan bicicletas?
I've got a flat tyre.	Tengo una llanta ponchada.
I came off my bike.	Me he caído de la bici.
bike	la bici(cleta)
brakes	los frenos
to cycle	andar en bicicleta
gear stick	el cambio de marchas
handlebars	la manivela
helmet	el casco
to hire	alquilar
inner tube	el neumático
lights	las luces
mountain bike	la bicicleta montañera
padlock	el candado
pump	la bomba/el inflador
puncture	el hueco/la ponchadura
racing bike	la bicicleta de carreras
saddle	el asiento
wheel	la rueda

ALOJAMIENTO
ACCOMMODATION

The range of accommodation available to travellers in Costa Rica is immense. The cheapest places to stay are **cabinas**. From expensive eco-lodges, to five-star hotels, to cabinas that are little more than concrete bunkers or made from palm fronds or corrugated tin – you can find it all. Most inexpensive places don't provide soap or towels, but almost always provide sheets.

In some towns, such as Quepos, there exists a glut of hotels that can be overwhelming. Take your time and examine what you'll be paying for. Most hotels will offer a discount if you are staying for more than three nights.

Is there a place to stay here?	**¿Hay un hotel por aquí?**
Where's (a) ...?	**¿Dónde hay ...?**
cabins	**unas cabinas**
guesthouse	**una casa de huéspedes**
hostel	**una residencia;**
	un hospedaje
hotel	**un hotel**
youth hostel	**un albergue juvenil**
I'm looking for a ...	**Busco un ...**
cheap hotel	**hotel barato**
good hotel	**buen hotel**
nearby hotel	**hotel cercano**
What's the address?	**¿Cuál es la dirección?**
Could you write the address, please?	**¿Puede usted escribir la dirección, por favor?**

(For camping terms, see page 133.)

ACCOMMODATION

BOOKING AHEAD

RESERVANDO

There are three words commonly used for 'room' in Costa Rica – cuarto, habitación and dormitorio (which is usually shared with others). Note that cuarto and dormitorio are masculine, while habitación is feminine.

I'd like to book a room please.	Quisiera reservar un cuarto.
Do you have any rooms available?	¿Tiene habitaciones libres?
For (three) nights.	Para/Por (tres) noches.
How much is it per night/ person?	¿Cuánto cuesta por noche/ persona?
I'll be arriving at (two o'clock).	Llegaré a (las dos).
My name's ...	Me llamo ...
Does it include breakfast?	¿Incluye el desayuno?

CHECKING IN

REGISTRACIÓN

I've made a reservation.   He hecho una reservacíon.

I'd like ...	Quisiera ...
a single room	un cuarto sencillo/ individual
a double room	un cuarto doble
to share a dorm	compartir un dormitorio
It must be ...	Tiene que ser ...
light	luminosa/o
quiet	tranquila/o

RETIREMENT HOME OR HOSTEL?

Be careful when searching for lodging that you don't ask for a pension, as hotels are called in some other Latin American countries. In Costa Rica, a pension is usually a place where pensionados, 'retirees', stay. Unless you want to stay in a retirement home, you'd better ask for something else.

I want a room with (a) ...	Quiero una habitación con ...
bathroom	baño privado
double bed	cama matrimonial
shower	ducha
twin beds	dos camas
window	ventana
Can I see it?	¿Puedo verla/o?
Can I see the bathroom?	¿Puedo ver el baño?
Are there any others?	¿Hay otras/os?
Are there any cheaper rooms?	¿Hay cuartos más baratos?
Is there a discount for students/children?	¿Hay algún descuento para estudiantes/niños?
Is there a discount for (four) nights?	¿Hay un descuento para (cuatro) noches?
It's fine, I'll take it.	Bueno, la/lo alquilo.
Can I pay by credit card?	¿Puedo pagar con tarjeta de crédito?
Do you require a deposit?	¿Demanda un depósito?
I'm going to stay for ...	Me voy a quedar ...
one day	un día
two days	dos días
one week	una semana
I'm not sure how long I'm staying.	No sé cuánto tiempo me voy a quedar.

ACCOMMODATION

FORMS

date	fecha
date of birth	fecha de nacimiento
name	nombre
surname	apellido
signature	firma

REQUESTS & QUERIES

PREGUNTAS

Cerré la puerta y se me olvidaron las llaves a dentro

Do you have a safe?	¿Tiene una caja fuerte?
Where is the bathroom?	¿Dónde está el baño?
Can I use the kitchen?	¿Puedo usar la cocina?
Can I use the telephone?	¿Puedo usar el teléfono?
Is there a lift?	¿Hay un ascensor?
I've locked myself out of my room.	Cerré la puerta y se me olvidaron las llaves a dentro.
Do you change money here?	¿Se cambia dinero en este hotel?
Should I leave my key at reception?	¿Tengo que dejar la llave en la recepción?
Is there a message board?	¿Tienen ustedes pizarra de anuncios?
Can I leave a message?	¿Puedo dejar un mensaje?
Is there a message for me?	¿Hay algún mensaje por mí?
Can I get my letters sent here?	¿Puedo recibir cartas aquí?
The key for room (10) please.	La llave de la habitación (diez), por favor.
Please wake me up at (seven) o'clock.	Despiérteme a las (siete) por favor.
The room needs to be cleaned.	Hay que limpiar la habitación.
Please change the sheets.	Cambie las sábanas, por favor.
Can you give me an extra blanket, please? I'm cold.	¿Puede darme otra manta, por favor? Tengo frío.
Is there somewhere to wash clothes?	¿Hay algún lugar donde pueda lavar la ropa?

ACCOMMODATION

COMPLAINTS

It's too ...
   cold
   dark
   expensive
   noisy
   small
I can't open/close the window.

I don't like this room.
The toilet won't flush.

Can I change to another
   dormitory/room?

QUEJAS

Es ...
   fría
   demasiado oscura
   cara
   ruidosa
   demasiado chico
No puedo abrir/cerrar la
   ventana.
No me gusta esta habitación.
La cadena del baño no
   funciona.
¿Puede cambiarme a otro
   dormitorio/habitación?

CHECKING OUT

When do I/we have to check
   out?
I'm/We're leaving now.
I would like to pay the bill.
Can I leave my backpack at
   reception until tonight?
Please call a taxi for me.

SALIENDO DEL HOTEL

¿A qué hora tengo/tenemos
   dejar la habitación?
Me voy/Nos vamos ahora.
Quiero pagar la cuenta.
¿Puedo dejar mi mochila en la
   recepción hasta esta noche?
¿Puede llamar un taxi, por
   favor?

ACCOMMODATION

THEY MAY SAY

Lo siento, no tenemos nada libre.
   Sorry, we're full.
¿Cuánto tiempo se va a quedar?
   How long will you be staying?
Su tarjeta de socio, por favor.
   Your membership card, please.

¿Cuántas noches?	How many nights?
¿Tiene ...?	Do you have ...?
cedula de identificación	identification
pasaporte	a passport

ACCOMMODATION

I'll return ...	Voy a volver ...
tomorrow	mañana
in a few days	en unos días

SIGNS

ALBERGUE JUVENIL	YOUTH HOSTEL
CABINAS	CABINS
CASA DE HUÉSPEDES	GUESTHOUSE
CUARTOS/HABITACIONES	ROOMS
HOSTERÍA/POSADA	INN
REFUGIO DE MONTAÑA	MOUNTAIN LODGE
RESIDENCIA	BUDGET HOTEL

RENTING / ALQUILANDO

Do you have any flats to rent?	¿Tiene apartamentos en alquiler?
I'm looking for a flat to rent for (three) months.	Estoy buscando un apartamento para alquilar por (tres) meses.
I'm here about your advertisement for a room to rent.	He venido por la habitación que anuncian para alquilar.

I'm looking for something close to the ...

Busco algo cerca ...

beach	de la playa
city centre	del centro de la ciudad
railway station	de la estación

Is there anything cheaper?	¿Hay algo más barato?
Could I see it?	¿Puedo verla/o?
How much is it per week/month?	¿Cuánto vale por semana/mes?
Do you require a deposit?	¿Tengo que dejar un depósito?
I'd like to rent the room for (one month).	Me gustaría alquilar la habitación por (un mes).

EN LA CIUDAD/ EL PUEBLO

AROUND TOWN

LOOKING FOR ...

I'm looking for a/the ...

BUSCANDO ...

Estoy buscando ...

art gallery	el museo; la galería de arte
bank	un banco
cinema	el cine
city centre	el centro de la ciudad
consulate	el consulado
... embassy	la embajada ...
main square	la plaza mayor
market	el mercado
museum	el museo
police	la policía/poli; el paco
post office	correos; el correo
public telephone	un teléfono público
public toilet	servicios; baños públicos
telephone center	la central telefónica
tourist information office	la oficina de turismo

What time does it open/close?   ¿A qué hora abre/cierra?

AT THE BANK

EN EL BANCO

The major problem with banking in rural Costa Rica is simply finding a bank. Sometimes it's necessary to take a bus to a larger town, or just plan ahead and bring cash. Most larger stores will change US dollars for Costa Rican colones, but a travelers cheque will need to be changed at a bank, tourist shop or large hotel.

Once encountered, bank services are pretty good, with automatic teller machines (ATMs) and money exchange. It's best to go early in the morning as banks sometimes close early and can run out of cash. Sometimes after a power-outage, which are common, ATMs don't reset correctly, so never leave banking to the last minute.

AROUND TOWN

Where can I change money?	¿Dónde puedo cambiar dinero?
Can I exchange money here?	¿Puedo cambiar dinero aquí?
Can I use my credit card to withdraw some money?	¿Puedo usar mi tarjeta de crédito para sacar dinero?
I want to exchange some money/travelers cheques.	Quiero cambiar dinero/cheques de viajero.
What's the exchange rate?	¿Cómo es el cambio?
How many colónes per (dollar)?	¿A cuánto está el (dólar)?
What's your commission?	¿Cuál es su comisión?
The ATM has swallowed my credit card.	El cajero automático se comió mi tarjeta de crédito.
Can I have money transferred here from my bank?	¿Puede usted transferir dinero de mi banco?
How long will it take to arrive?	¿Cuánto tiempo tardará en llegar?
Has my money arrived yet?	¿Ha llegado mi dinero?
Can I transfer money overseas?	¿Puedo enviar dinero al extranjero?
Where do I sign?	¿Dónde firmo?

MONEY, MONEY, MONEY

Just as in English speaking countries, Costa Rican people have a variety of slang terms for their money, the Colón.

teja	100 Colones	can also mean '100' in general
media teja	50 Colones	(lit: half teja)
rojo/pargo	1000 Colones	rojo means 'red' and pargo is a 'red snapper' – both names refer to the red color of the bill
tucán	5000 Colones	this bill has a picture of a colorful toucan

Automatic Teller Machine (ATM)	el cajero automático
(bank) notes	los billetes/recibos (de banco)
cashier	la caja
coins	las monedas; los colones
credit card	la tarjeta de crédito
exchange	el cambio
identification	la identificación
signature	la firma

AROUND TOWN

AT THE POST OFFICE	EN LA OFICINA DE CORREOS
I'd like to send a ...	Quisiera enviar ...
letter	una carta
parcel	un paquete
postcard	una postal
telegram	un telegrama
I'd like some stamps.	Quisiera unas estampillas.
How much is the postage?	¿Cuanto cuestan las estampillas?
How much does it cost to send this to (London)?	¿Cuánto me cuesta enviar esto a (Londres)?
Is there any mail for me?	¿Hay alguna carta para mí?
air mail	por vía aérea
envelope	un sobre
express mail	el correo rápido
mail box	el buzón
parcel	un paquete
pen	el lapicero; la pluma
postcode	el código postal
registered mail	el correo certificado
surface mail	por vía terrestre; marítima

WHAT IS?

What is this?	¿Qué es esto?
What is happening?	¿Qué pasa?
What happened?	¿Qué pasó?
What is s/he doing?	¿Qué está haciendo?
What do you charge?	¿Cuánto cobra?
How much is it?	¿Cuánto vale?
Can I have one please?	Quisiera una/o, por favor.

TELECOMMUNICATIONS   TELECOMUNICACIONES

The phone system in Costa Rica has improved dramatically in recent times. You can access international operators and calling cards from many public telephones or in communications offices. Otherwise, you have to purchase calling cards, which are reasonably priced.

Local calls can also be made at communications offices or on phones in public establishments, and you'll be charged afterwards according to the length of the call. Some small towns only have one or two telephones. All of Costa Rica falls under the same area code (506), so all domestic calls are at a local rate and inexpensive.

I want to make a call.	Quiero hacer una llamada.
I want to ring (Australia).	Quiero llamar a (Australia).
How much does a three-minute call cost?	¿Cuánto cuesta una llamada de tres minutos?
How much does each extra minute cost?	¿Cuánto cuesta cada minuto adicional?
The number is ...	El número es ...
What's the area code for ...?	¿Cuál es el código de ...?
I want to make a reverse-charge phone call.	Quiero hacer una llamada a cobrar.
It's engaged.	Está ocupado.
I've been cut off.	Me han cortado (la llamada).
operator	la/el operador(a)
phone book	la guía telefónica
phone box	la cabina telefónica
phonecard	la tarjeta de teléfono
telephone	el teléfono
telephone office	la central telefónica

Internet

Internet

There are currently Internet cafes in San José, Heredia, San Isidro and most major tourist destinations, with new locations opening all the time.

How can I get ... access?	¿Cómo puedo accesar a ...?
email	correo electronico
Internet	Internet
Is there a local Internet ...?	¿Hay algún ... de Internet?
café	café
service	servicio local
I need to check my email.	Tengo que chequear mi correo electrónico.
Is there a cheap rate for ...?	¿Hay alguna tarifa más barata ...?
evenings	para las llamadas nocturnas
weekends	durante los fines de semana

Making a Call

Haciendo una llamada telefonica

Hello! (making a call)	¡Hola!
Hello! (answering a call)	¿Diga?
Can I speak to (Angel)?	¿Está (Angel)?
Who's calling?	¿De parte de quién?
It's (Susana).	De (Susana).
Just a minute, I'll put her/him on.	Un momento, ya te la/lo pongo.
I'm sorry, s/he's not here.	Lo siento, pero ahora no está.
What time will s/he be back?	¿A qué hora volverá?
Yes, please tell her/him I called.	Sí, por favor, dile que he llamado.
No, thanks, I'll call back later.	No gracias, llamaré más tarde.

AROUND TOWN

SIGHTSEEING

Do you have a local map?	¿Tiene una mapa de la ciudad?
What are the main attractions?	¿Cuáles son las atracciones principales?
What's that?	¿Qué es eso?
How old is it?	¿Qué viejo es?; ¿De cuándo es?
Can I take photographs?	¿Puedo tomar fotos?
Is there an admission charge?	¿Hay que pagar?
Is there a discount for ...?	¿Hay descuentos para ...?
children	niños
pensioners	pensionados
students	estudiantes

TURISMO

SIGNS

ABIERTO	OPEN
BAÑOS	TOILETS
CALIENTE/FRÍO	HOT/COLD
CERRADO	CLOSED
ENTRADA	ENTRANCE
ENTRADA GRATIS	FREE ADMISSION
CHEQUEO DE EQUIPAJE	CHECK-IN COUNTER
INFORMACIÓN	INFORMATION
NO TOCAR	DO NOT TOUCH
NO (USAR EL) FLASH	DO NOT USE FLASH
PROHIBIDO ...	NO ...
COMER	EATING
EL PASO	ENTRY
FUMAR	SMOKING
TOMAR FOTOS	PHOTOGRAPHY
RESERVADO	RESERVED
SALIDA (DE EMERGENCIA)	(EMERGENCY) EXIT
SERVICIOS	TOILETS
TELÉFONO	TELEPHONE

AROUND TOWN

GUIDED TOURS   ## TURISMO CON GUÍA

GUIDED TOURS	TURISMO CON GUÍA
Do you organize group tours?	¿Organizan excursiones en grupo?
What type of people go on the tour?	¿Qué tipo de gente participa?
Will I have free time?	¿Voy a tener tiempo libre?
How long will we stop for?	¿Cuánto tiempo vamos a parar?
What time do I have to be back?	¿A qué hora tengo que volver?
The guide has paid.	La/El guía ha pagado.
I'm with them.	Voy con ellos.
I've lost my group.	He perdido mi grupo.
Have you seen a group of (Australians)?	¿Ha visto usted un grupo de (australianos)?

SALIENDO GOING OUT

There's usually plenty to do at night in San José and the more touristy areas of Costa Rica, although the nightlife is still modest compared to most other capital cities and tourist areas. From the packed university bar district in San Pedro just outside San José, to very raucous reggae bars in Puerto Viejo, to quasi-raves in Tamarindo, to alcohol-driven salsa clubs in Quepos, you'll definitely find nightlife.

In many traditional towns and less tourist-oriented places, however, you may have to settle for a quiet night playing pool and sipping on an Imperial, or simply hanging out with friends and turning in early like many of the locals.

WHERE TO GO

What's there to do in the
   evenings?
What's on tonight?
Where can I find out
   what's on?

I feel like going to a/the ...
   bar
   café
   cinema
   concert
   disco
   opera
   restaurant
   theatre

LUGARES PARA SALIR

¿Qué se puede hacer por
   las noches?
¿Qué hay esta noche?
¿Dónde puedo averiguar qué
   hay esta noche?

Tengo ganas de ir ...
   a un bar
   a una soda
   al cine
   a un concierto
   a una discoteca
   a la ópera
   a un restaurante
   al teatro

THE PARTY   LA FIESTA

More than going out to bars and nightclubs, private parties or
fiestas are the best alternative for meeting people, dancing and
getting to the heart of Costa Rican life. It's almost guaranteed that
anyone you get to know in a smaller town will invite you to one at
some stage.

I brought something to drink.	Traje algo para tomar.
Have we run out of alcohol?	¿Se acabó el licor?
I want to dance.	Quiero bailar.
How do you dance this?	¿Como se baila esto?
What sort of music is this?	¿Que clase de música es esta?

bolero	unlike the fast bolero of Spain, the Latin American version is slow and romantic
calypso	lilting, upbeat music originally from Trinidad. An influence of reggae.
cha cha cha	related to **mambo**, the Cuban 1950s cha cha cha developed the off-beat step to include a quick change of step on the last two beats of the rhythm; said to have been designed specifically to appeal to white dancers
cueca	also known as the **marinera** and the **cueca** originated as a folk dance in Chile, north Argentina and Peru
cumbia	Afro-Caribbean rhythm
habanera	a dance which developed in Cuba in the late 19th century. It's slow and provocative, and accompanied by high-pitched singing reminiscent of flamenco.

mambo	ballroom dance of Cuban origin, performed as an off-beat rumba
merengue	originating in the French-speaking Caribbean, it is always danced with the weight on one foot, thus creating a limp-like movement
techno-merengue	merengue set to a fast, danceable, techno beat. Very popular in night clubs.
pasodoble	a fast dance in double time
ranchera	Mexican country music
reggae	originally from Jamaica, this rhythmic music has spread from the Caribbean coast across Costa Rica
rumba	a dance style of Afro-Cuban origin in which the rhythm is provided by maracas 'drums', and a singer; known for its erotic side-to-side hip movements
salsa	developed in New York, and popular in the Caribbean in the 1960s and 1970s, the catchy salsa is a mix of son and other Latin American rhythms
samba	of Brazilian origin, with an African influence, the samba is a lively ballroom dance in double time
son	the Cuban equivalent of American country music
tango	originally a fast, sensual dance which developed in Argentina in the 1880s, it became a more slow, melancholy dance in the 1920s
vallenato	based on the European piano accordian

GOING OUT

INVITES

What are you doing this ...?
  evening
  weekend

Would you like to go for a ...?
  drink
  meal

Do you know a good
  restaurant (that's cheap)?
My shout (I'll buy). (inf)
Do you want to come to
  the (Los Illegales)
  concert with me?

INVITACIONES

¿Qué hace ...?
  esta noche
  este fin de semana

¿Quiere salir a ...?
  tomar algo
  cenar

¿Conoce algún restaurante
  (que no sea muy caro)?
Te invito.
¿Quiere venir conmigo al
  concierto de (Los
  Illegales)?

Responding to Invites

Sure!
Yes, I'd love to.
OK. Where shall we go?
No, I can't.
What about tomorrow?

Contestando invitaciones

¡Por supuesto!
Me encantaría.
Sí, vamos. ¿Pero, dónde?
Lo siento pero no puedo.
¿Qué tal mañana?

Nightclubs & Bars

Are there any discos?
How much is it to get in?
Shall we dance?

Discotecas y bares

¿Hay alguna discoteca?
¿Cuánto cuesta la entrada?
¿Vamos a bailar?

THEY MAY SAY

Spanish has many words related to going out. All of
these verbs mean 'to go out and have a good time':

ir de copas	ir de farra
enfiestase	ir de rumba
ir(se) de fiesta	ir de pachanga

I'm sorry, I can't dance.	Lo siento, pero no puedo bailar.
Come on!	¡Venga, vamos!
What type of music do you like?	¿Qué tipo de música prefiere?
I really like (reggae).	Me encanta (el reggae).
Where can we dance some (salsa)?	¿Dónde se puede bailar (salsa)?
How much is the cover charge?	¿Cuánto vale/cuesta entrar?
Do you have to pay to enter the dance?	¡Hay que pagar para entrar al baile?
No, it's free.	No, es gratis.
Yes, it's (700) colones.	Sí, vale (setecientos) colones.
This place is great!	¡Este lugar me encanta!
I don't like the music here.	No me gusta la música.
Do you want to go somewhere else?	¿Vamos a otro sitio?

ARRANGING TO MEET

ENCONTRANDO

What time shall we meet?	¿A qué hora quedamos?
Where shall we meet?	¿Dónde nos encontramos?
Let's meet at (eight o'clock) in the (Parque Central).	Nos encontramos a las (ocho) en la (Parque Central).
OK!	¡Bien!
OK. I'll see you then.	De acuerdo. Nos vemos.
I'll come over at (six).	Vendré a las (seis).
I'll pick you (inf) up at (nine).	Te recogeré a las (nueve).
I'll try to make it.	Intentaré venir.
If I'm not there by (nine), don't wait for me.	Si no estoy a las (nueve), no me espere.
I'll be along later. Where will you (pl) be?	¡Llegaré más tarde. Dónde van a estar?
See you later/tomorrow.	Hasta luego/mañana.
Sorry I'm late.	Siento llegar tarde.
Never mind.	No importa; No pasa nada.

DATING & ROMANCE
The Date

Would you (inf) like to do something ...?
  tonight
  tomorrow
  at the weekend

Yes, I'd love to.
Sorry, but I'm busy.

Where would you like to go?
Will you take me home?
Do you want to come inside for a while?
Can I see you again?

Can I call you?
I'll call you tomorrow.
Goodnight.

Making Love

I (don't) like that.
Please stop!

SALIENDO JUNTOS Y ROMANCE
La cita

¿Quieres hacer algo ...?

  esta noche
  mañana
  este fin de semana

Me encantaría.
Desculpe pero estoy ocupada/o.

¿Dónde quieres ir?
¿Me acompañas a casa?
¿Quieres entrar por un ratito?

¿Quieres que nos veamos de nuevo?
¿Puedo llamarte?
Te llamaré mañana.
Buenas noches.

Haciendo el amor

Eso (no) me gusta.
¡Para por favor!;
¡No sigas, por favor!

INTIMATE SPANISH

cock	picha	to masturbate	masturbarse
cuddle	brazo	oral sex	sexo oral
erection	erección	orgasm	orgasmo
to fuck	culiar	pussy	pinocha
kiss	beso	safe sex	sexo sano
to lick	lamer	sexy	sexy
lover	amante	to suck	mamar/chupar

GOING OUT

CLASSIC PICK-UP LINES

Would you like a (drink)?	¿Quiere algo para tomar?
Do you have a light?	¿Tiene fuego, por favor?
Do you (inf) mind if I sit here?	¿Te importa si me siento aquí?
Do you have a girlfriend/ boyfriend?	¿Tiene novia/o?
Can I take you (inf)home?	¿Puedo llevarte a casa?

Please don't stop!	¡Sigue!; ¡Por favor, no pare!
I think we should stop now.	Creo que deberíamos parar.
Kiss me!	¡Dame un beso!
Take this off.	Sácate/Quítate esto.
Touch me (here).	Tócame (aquí).
I want to make love to you.	Quiero hacerte el amor.
Let's go to bed!	¡Vámonos a la cama!
Do you have a condom?	¿Tienes un condón/ preservativo?
Let's use a condom.	Quiero que usemos un condón.

INTIMATE BODY

I really like your ...	Me encanta(n) tu(s) ...
body	cuerpo
breasts	tetas
bum/ass	culo/cola/nalgas/trasero
chest (male)	pecho
eyes	ojos
hair	cabello/pelo
hands	manos
lips	labios
mouth	boca
skin	piel

Afterwards / Después

That was great.
Estuvo fantastico.

Can I stay over?
¿Puedo quedarme a pasar la noche?

You can't sleep here tonight.
No puedes quedarte aquí esta noche.

When can I see you again?
¿Podemos vernos alguna otra vez?

I'll call you.
Ya te llamaré.

Love / Amor

I love you.
Te quiero/amo.

I'm in love with you.
Estoy enamorada/o de ti.

I'm really happy with you.
Estoy muy feliz contigo.

Do you love me?
¿Me quieres/amas?

Do you want to go out with me?
¿Quieres salir conmigo?

Let's move in together.
¿Por qué no nos vamos a vivir juntos?

PURA VIDA

If there's one saying that embodies Costa Rican life, it's Pura Vida. Although this translates literally as, 'pure life', it's actually a more profound concept expressing positivity, harmony and well-being – something, but not quite, like 'right on' in English.

Very similar to pura vida in its meaning, the saying tuanis is becoming increasingly popular, especially with younger generations. Rumour has it that North American expatriates living in Costa Rica in the 1960s and 1970s would frequently say 'too nice' to explain how they were feeling. 'Too nice' was adopted by Spanish speakers and transformed into tuanis.

GOING OUT

CLASSIC REJECTIONS

No thanks.	No, gracias.
I'm here with my girlfriend/ boyfriend.	Estoy aquí con mi novia/o.
Stop hassling me.	Por favor, deje de molestarme.
Leave me alone!	¡Déjeme en paz!
Excuse me, I have to go now.	Lo siento, pero tengo que irme.
Get lost!	¡Vete!; ¡Hasta nunca!

Leaving & Breaking Up

Undespidiendo y el fin del relación

I have to leave tomorrow.	Tengo que irme mañana.
I'll miss you.	Te extrañaré; Te voy a echar de menos.
I'll come and visit you.	Vendré a visitarte.
I really want us to keep in touch.	Me gustaría que nos mantuviéramos en contacto.
I don't think it's working out.	Creo que la relación no está funcionando.
I want to remain friends.	Me gustaría que quedáramos como amigos.

LA FAMILIA   FAMILY

QUESTIONS   PREGUNTAS

Are you married?   ¿Está casada/o?
Do you have a girlfriend/   ¿Tiene novia/o?
  boyfriend?
How many children do you   ¿Cuántos hijos tiene?
  have?
How many brothers/sisters   ¿Cuántas/os hermanas/os
  do you have?   tiene?
How old are they?   ¿Cuántos años tienen?
Do you get along with your   ¿Te llevas bien con tu
  (inf) family?   familia?

REPLIES   RESPUESTAS

I'm ...
  single   Soy soltera/o.
  married   Estoy casada/o.
  separated   Estoy separada/o.
  divorced   Estoy divorciada/o.
  a widow/widower   Soy viuda/o.

I have a partner.   Tengo una compañera/o.
We live together but we're not Vivimos juntos pero no
  married.   estamos casados.
I don't have any children.   No tengo hijos.
I have a daughter/son.   Tengo una hija/un hijo.
I live with my family.   Vivo con mi familia.

FAMILY MEMBERS   FAMILIARES

baby   el bebé
boy   el chico; muchacho
brother   el hermano; herma (col)
children   los hijos
Christian name   el nombre cristiano

79

FAMILY

dad	el papá
daughter	la hija
family	la familia
father	el padre
father-in-law	el suegro
girl	la chica/muchacha
grandmother/grandfather	la abuela; el abuelo
husband	el esposo/marido
mother	la madre
mother-in-law	la suegra
mum	la mamá
nickname	el apodo
sister	la hermana
son	el hijo
wife	la esposa/mujer

TALKING WITH PARENTS

HABLANDO CON PADRES

When's the baby due?	¿Cuándo espera el bebé?
What are you going to call the baby?	¿Cómo se va a llamar el bebé?
Is this your first child?	¿Es su primer bebé?
How many children do you have?	¿Cuántos hijos tiene?
How old are your ...?	¿Cuántos años tienen sus ...?
children (female)	hijas
children (male or both sexes)	hijos
I can't believe it! You look too young.	¡No lo puedo creer! Parece tan joven.
Does s/he attend school?	¿Va a la escuela?
Who looks after the children?	¿Quién se cuida de hijas/hijos?
Do you have grandchildren?	¿Tiene nietos?
What's the baby's name?	¿Cómo se llama el bebé?
Is it a boy or a girl?	¿Es niña o niño?
Is s/he well-behaved?	¿Se porta bien?

FAMILY

Does s/he let you (inf) sleep at night?	¿Te deja dormir por las noches?
S/he's very big for her/his age!	¡Está muy grande para su edad!
What a beautiful child!	¡Es un(a) niña/o preciosa/o!
S/he looks like you (inf).	Se parece a ti.
S/he has your eyes.	Tiene sus ojos.
Who does s/he look like, Mum or Dad?	¿A quién ha salido, al padre o a la madre?

TALKING WITH CHILDREN

HABLANDO CON NIÑOS

What's your name?	¿Cómo te llamas?
How old are you?	¿Cuántos años tienes?
When's your birthday?	¿Cuándo es tu cumpleaños?
Have you got brothers and sisters?	¿Tienes hermanos y hermanas?
Do you have a pet at home?	¿Tienes alguna mascota?
Do you go to school or kinder?	¿Vas a la escuela o al kinder?
Is your teacher nice?	¿Es simpática/o tu maestra/o?
Do you like school?	¿Te gusta ir a la escuela?
Do you play sport?	¿Practicas algún deporte?
What sport do you play?	¿Qué deporte practicas?
What do you do after school?	¿Qué haces después de la escuela?
Do you study English?	¿Estudias inglés?
We speak a different language in my country so I don't understand you very well.	En mi país hablamos otra lengua diferente y por eso no te entiendo bien.
I come from very far away.	Vengo de muy lejos.
Do you want to play a game?	¿Quieres jugar conmigo?
What shall we play?	¿A qué jugamos?
Have you lost your parents?	¿Has perdido a tus padres?

FAMILY

PETS   MASCOTAS

In Costa Rica, people often name their pets after a friend, either out of respect or as a joke.

Do you like animals?	¿Te gustan los animales?
What a cute (puppy)!	¡Qué (cachorrito) más lindo!
What's s/he called?	¿Cómo se llama?
Is it female or male?	¿Es hembra o macho?
How old is s/he?	¿Cuánto tiempo tiene?
Does s/he bite?	¿Muerde?

I have a ...	Tengo ...
bird	un pájaro
canary	un canario
cat	un(a) gata/o
dog	un perro/cachorro
fish	un pez
guinea pig	un quilo
hamster	una quila
kitten	un(a) gatita/o
mouse	un ratón
puppy	un cachorro/cachorrito
rabbit	un conejo
tortoise	una tortuga

INTERESES   INTERESTS

COMMON INTERESTS

What do you do in your spare time?

Do you like ...?
I (don't) like ...
  basketball
  dancing
  diving (scuba)
  diving (snorkeling)
  films
  food
  football
  hiking

  music
  reading
  shopping
  skiing
  surfing
  swimming
  traveling

INTERESES COMUNES

¿Qué le gusta hacer en tu tiempo libre?

¿Te gusta ...?
(No) me gusta ...
  el baloncesto/basket
  bailar
  bucear
  esnorkelar
  el cine
  la comida
  el fútbol
  el excursionismo/
    la caminata
  la música
  leer
  ir de compras
  esquiar
  surfear/sorfear
  nadar
  viajar

STAYING IN TOUCH

Tomorrow is my last day here.
Do you have a pen and paper?
What's your address?
Here's my address.
If you ever visit (Scotland) you must come and visit us.

If you come to (Melbourne) you've got a place to stay.
Do you have an email address?

CORRESPONDENCIA

Mañana es mi último día aquí.
¿Tiene papel y lapicero?
¿Cuál es su dirección?
Ésta es mi dirección.
Si alguna vez visite a (Escocia) tiene que venir a vistarnos.

Si venga a (Melbourne) tiene un lugar para quedar.
¿Tiene correo electrónico?

Do you have access to a fax?	¿Tiene acceso a fax?
I'll send you (inf) copies of the photos.	Te enviaré copias de las fotos.
Don't forget to write! (inf)	¡No te olvides de escribirme!
It's been great meeting you.	Gusto en conocerle.
Keep in touch!	¡Nos mantendremos en contacto!

Writing   Escribiendo

If you want to contact your new friends by writing to them in Spanish when you get back home, here are some useful words and phrases.

Costa Ricans often end a letter with un abrazo, 'a hug' or un beso, 'a kiss' for closer friends. A simple cordialmente, 'cordially', usually works for more casual friends.

Dear ...	*Querida/o ...*
I'm sorry it's taken me so long to write.	*Siento haber tardado tanto en escribir.*
It was great to meet you (sg/pl).	*Gusto conocerle/conocerlos.*
Thank you so much for your (sg/pl) *hospitality.*	*Muchísimas gracias por tu/su hospitalidad.*
I miss you (sg/pl).	*Te/Los echo mucho de menos.*
I had a fantastic time in Costa Rica.	*Lo pasé muy bien en Costa Rica.*
My favourite place was ...	*Mi lugar preferido fue ...*
I hope to visit Costa Rica again soon.	*Espero pronto visitar de nuevo a Costa Rica.*
Say 'hi' to (Isabel) and (Miguel) for me!	*Saluda a (Isabel) y a (Miguel) de mi parte.*
I'd love to see you (sg/pl) *again.*	*Tengo ganas de verle/verlos otra vez.*
Write soon!	*¡Escríbeme pronto!*
With love,	*Un beso; Besos; Un abrazo,*
Regards,	*Cordialmente,*

INTERESTS

ART
Seeing Art

ARTE
Viendo arte

When's the gallery open?	¿A qué hora abren el museo/la galería?
What's in the collection?	¿Qué hay en la colección?
What kind of art are you (inf) interested in?	¿Qué tipo de arte te interesa?
I'm interested in ...	Me interesa(n) ...
animation	los dibujos animados; las fabulas (col)
cyber art	el arte cibernético
design	el diseño
graphic art	el arte gráfico
painting	la pintura
performance art	el arte de representación
Renaissance art	el arte del renacimiento
Romanesque art	el arte románico
sculpture	la escultura

INTERESTS

Many other words associated with art styles are similar to English. For instance, baroque is **barroco**

building	el edificio
church	la iglesia
curator	un(a) conservador(a)
epoch	la época
etching	el aguafuerte/guaro
permanent collection	una exposición permanente
photographer	la/el fotógrafa/o
a print	un grabado
sculptor	un(a) escultor(a)
souvenir shop	la tienda de recuerdos/souvenirs
statue	una estatua

INTERESTS

MALA NOTA

Mala nota basically means that something's not cool, so if you say ¡Qué mala nota!, it means 'how uncool', or 'that's bad'.

Opinions

I like the works of ...
What do you think of ...?
It's not as good as ...
It's reminiscent of ...

It's ...
    awful
    beautiful
    dramatic
    incomprehensible
    interesting
    marvellous
    unusual

Opiñones

Me gustan las obras de ...
¿Cómo le parece ...?
No es tan bueno como ...
Me recuerda a ...

Es ...
    horrible
    bonito
    dramático
    incomprensible
    interesante
    maravilloso
    extraño

BAD SPANISH – CURSES

¡Condenado!	Damn!
¡Dios mio!	My God!
¡Hijo de puta!	Son of a bitch!
¡No me jodas!	Don't fuck with me!
¡Maldita sea!	Fucking hell!
¡Me cago en dios!	Christ! (serious) (lit: I shit on God)
¡Mierda!	Shit!
¡Que bruto!	How rude!
¡Que cagada!; ¡Carajo!	Shit!
¡Vete a la mierda!	Go to hell! (lit: go to shit)

MUSIC
Latin American Music

Although all these types of music can be heard in Costa Rica, the most popular are **salsa**, **merengue** (or **techno-merengue**), **reggae**, **cumbia**, **disco** (pop), **romántico**, and **rock latino**. See the chapter on 'Going Out', page 70, for more information on music.

Andean

Andean music employs a number of interesting instruments. The **charango** is similar to a ukulele, while the **violín chapaco** is a variation of the European violin. Instruments of pre-Columbian origin are typically woodwind instruments, such as the **quena**, 'reed flute' and the **zampoña**, 'pan flute'. The breathy lead instruments of the rural altiplano are the **tarka** and the **sikuri**. Drums include the **caja** (tambourine-like) and the **huankara**.

Colombian Andean music has been strongly influenced by music from Spain. Typical forms are the **bambuco**, **pasillo** and **torbellino**, all of which use stringed instruments.

cumbia

a rhythmic Afro-Caribbean music

MÚSICA
Música Latina Americana

INTERESTS

¡BUENA NOTA! – COOL!	
Es/Está ...	It's ...
buena nota	cool
buenísima/o	great; right on!
extraordinaria/o	amazing
fantastica/o	fantastic
loca/o	crazy
malismo	terrible
pura vida	cool; right on!
tuanis	cool; right on!

INTERESTS

disco (Pop)

much of this music is similar to standard international pop, but often with a salsa or merengue influence. Some of it simply is international pop.

mariachi

perhaps the most 'typical' Mexican music, with a heavy portion of brass. There are many mariachis in downtown San José.

merengue (techno-merengue)

a very danceable music originating from the French-speaking Caribbean. **Techno-merengue** has a fast techno-beat.

música Criolla

with its roots in Spain and Africa, its main instruments are guitars and a **cajón** (wooden box used as a drum)

reggae

the reggae influence is felt throughout the Caribbean coast of Central American, and more danceable reggae (often with an added techno beat) is popular across Costa Rica

rock latino

while influenced by rock music, this form of rock is usually a bit more upbeat and often includes horns

romántico

a slower, yes, you guessed it, romantic music popular with older generations

salsa

dance music which spread through the Caribbean in the 1960s

tango

this famous music and dance of Buenos Aires is ever-popular

What music do you like?	¿Qué tipo de música te gusta?
Which bands do you like?	¿Qué grupos le gustan?
I like (the) ...	Me gustan (los) ...
Have you heard the latest record by ...?	¿Ha escuchado lo último de ...?
Which station plays salsa?	¿En qué emisora/estación de radio ponen salsa?

Which is a good station for (jazz)?	¿Qué emisora/estación de radio es buena para escuchar (jazz)?
What frequency is it on?	¿En qué frecuencia está?
Where can you hear traditional music around here?	¿Dónde se puede escuchar música folklórica en esta ciudad?
Where shall we sit?	¿Dónde nos sentamos?
What a fantastic concert!	¡Qué concierto más fantástico!
It's terrible!	¡Es terrible!
This singer's brilliant.	Esta/e cantante es fabulosa/o.

See also On Tour, page 171.

INTERESTS

CINEMA & THEATRE

EL CINE Y EL TEATRO

I feel like going to a(n) ...	Tengo ganas de ir ...
ballet	al ballet
comedy	a una comedia
film	al cine
play	al teatro
What's on at the cinema tonight?	¿Qué película dan en el cine esta noche?
Are there any tickets for ...?	¿Hay entradas para ...?
Sorry, we're sold out.	Lo siento pero se han agotado las entradas/ticketes.
Is it in English?	¿Es en inglés?
Does it have English subtitles?	¿Tiene subtítulos en inglés?
Is there a short before the film?	¿Hay algún corto antes de la película?
Are those seats taken?	¿Están libres estos asientos?
Have you seen ...?	¿Ha visto ...?
Have you seen the latest film by (Litín)?	¿Ha visto la última película de (Litín)?

INTERESTS

Who's in it?	¿Quién actúa?
It stars ...	Actúa ...
Who's it by?	¿Quién la dirige?
It's directed by ...	La dirige ...
It's been really well reviewed.	La han criticado muy bien.

I (don't) like ...	(No) me gusta/n ...
action movies	las películas de acción
amateur film	el cine aficionado
animated films	las películas de dibujos animados; las fabulas (col)
art films	el arte y ensayo
black comedy	la comedia negra
classical theatre	el teatro clásico
comedy	la comedia
documentary	los documentales
drama	el drama
film noir	el cine negro
horror movies	el cine de terror
period dramas	el cine de época
realism	el cine realista
sci-fi movies	el cine de ciencia ficción
short films	los cortos
thrillers	el cine de suspenso
war films	el cine de guerra

BAD SPANISH – INSULTS

¡Cara de picha!	Dick face!
¡Carajo!	Prick/Asshole!
¡Grosero!	Slob!
¡Mamador de picha!	Cock sucker!
¡Pendejo!	Loser/Jerk!
¡Puta/o!	Whore/Asshole!

Opinions

Did you like the ...?
 film
 performance
 play

I liked it very much.
I didn't like it very much.

I thought it was ...
 excellent
 OK

I had a few problems with the language.

Opiñones

¿Le ha gustado la/el ...?
 película
 actuación
 obra

Me ha gustado mucho.
No me ha gustado mucho.

Creo que ha sido ...
 fantástica/o
 regular

He tenido dificultades para entender la lengua.

INTERESTS

LITERATURE

Who's your favourite author?

I read ...
I've read everything by ...
I prefer the works of ...
What kind of books do you (inf) read?

I (don't) like ...
 the classics
 comics
 crime/detective novels
 fantasy literature
 fiction
 non-fiction
 novels
 poetry
 romance
 science-fiction
 short stories
 travel writing

LITERATURA

¿Quién es su autor(a) favorita/o?

Leo mucho a ...
Lo he leído todo de ...
Prefiero las obras de ...
¿Qué tipo de libros lees?

(No) me gusta(n) ...
 la literatura clásica
 los cómics
 la novela negra
 la literatura fantástica
 la ficción
 el ensayo
 las novelas
 la poesía
 la literatura romántica
 la ciencia ficción
 los cuentos
 los libros de viajes

Have you read ...?	¿Ha leído ...?
What did you think of ...?	¿Qué le pareció ...?
Can you recommend a book for me?	¿Me puede recomendar algún libro?

Opinions
Opiñones

I thought it was ...	Creo que es ...
boring	aburrido
entertaining	entretenido

I thought it was ...	Me pareció ...
badly written	muy mal escrito
better/worse than her/his last book	mejor/peor que su libro anterior
well-written	bien escrita/o

INTERESTS

CARMEN NARANJO

One of the most well-known Costa Rican writers is the prizewinning novelist, poet and short-story writer Carmen Naranjo. Her works have been translated into several languages including English.

HOBBIES
INTERESES

Do you have any hobbies?	¿Tiene algún pasatiempo?

I like ...	Me gusta ...
gardening	la jardinería
travelling	viajar

I like to ...	Me gusta ...
cook	cocinar
draw	dibujar
paint	pintar
sew	coser
take photographs	sacar fotos

I make ...	Hago ...
jewellery	joyería
pottery	cerámica
I collect ...	Colecciono ...
books	libros
coins	monedas
comics	cómics/caricaturas
dolls	muñecas
miniature cars	carritos
stamps	estampillas

TALKING ABOUT TRAVELLING

HABLANDO SOBRE VIAJANDO

INTERESTS

Have you travelled much?	¿Ha viajado mucho?
How long have you been travelling?	¿Cuánto tiempo lleva viajando?
I've been travelling for (two) months.	Hace (dos) meses que estoy viajando.
Where have you been?	¿Dónde ha estado?
I've been to ...	He estado en ...
What did you think of (Monteverde)?	¿Cómo le pareció (Monteverde)?
I thought it was ...	Me pareció ...
great	fantástica/o
OK	más o menos
too expensive	demasiado cara/o
boring	aburrida/o
horrible	horrible
There are too many tourists there.	Hay demasiados turistas.
Not many people speak (English).	Poca gente habla (inglés).
I was ripped off in (San José).	Me robaron en (San José).

People are really friendly there.	Allá la gente es muy amable.
What's there to do in (Quepos)?	¿Qué se puede hacer en (Quepos)?
The best time to go is in (December).	La mejor época para ir es (diciembre).
Is it expensive?	¿Es caro?
Is it safe for women travellers on their own?	¿Es seguro para mujeres que viajan solas?

THEY MAY SAY

(No) es importante.	It's (not) important.
(No) es posible.	It's (not) possible.
No es nada.	It's nothing.
No (me) importa.	It doesn't matter.
No problema.	It's no problem.

STARS
Astrology

I'm ...

- Aries
- Taurus
- Gemini
- Cancer
- Leo
- Virgo
- Libra
- Scorpio
- Sagittarius
- Capricorn
- Aquarius
- Pisces

ESTRELLAS
Astrología

Soy ...

- aries
- tauro
- géminis
- cáncer
- leo
- virgo
- libra
- escorpión
- sagitario
- capricornio
- acuario
- piscis

When's your birthday?	¿Cuándo es su cumpleaños?
What star sign are you?	¿De qué signo es?
I don't believe in astrology.	No creo en los signos del zodíaco.
I get on well with (Virgos).	Me llevo bien con los (virgo).
That explains it!	¡Eso lo explica todo!

(Leo's) are very ...   (Los leo) son muy ...

aggressive	agresivos
caring	bondadosos
charming	encantadores
crafty	habilidosos/ingeniosos
creative	creativos
emotional	emocionales
indecisive	indecisos
intense	intensos
interesting	interesantes
jealous	celosos
loyal	leales
outgoing	abiertos
passive	pasivos
proud	orgullosos
self-centred	egoístas
sensual	sensuales
stingy	tacaños

INTERESTS

ascendent	el ascendente
chart	la carta astral
descendent	el descendiente
horoscope	el horóscopo
personality	la personalidad
zodiac	el zodíaco

INTERESTS

Astronomy

Are you interested in astronomy?

I'm interested in astronomy.

Do you have a telescope?

Is there a planetarium/observatory nearby?

Where's the best place near here to see the night sky?

Will it be cloudy tonight?

Astronomía

¿Le interesa la astronomía?

Me interesa la astronomía.

¿Tiene un telescopio?

¿Hay algún observatorio por aquí cerca?

¿Cuál es el mejor lugar para observar el cielo de noche?

¿Va a estar nublado esta noche?

When can I see ...?
    Mars
    Mercury
    Pluto
    Uranus

What time does it rise?

What time will it set?

Can I see it at this time of year from here?

Which way is north?

Is that Orion?

It's the other way up in the southern/northern hemisphere.

¿Cuándo puedo ver ...?
    Marte
    Mercurio
    Plutón
    Urano

¿A qué hora sale?

¿A qué hora se pone?

¿Se puede ver en esta época del año desde aquí?

¿Dónde está el norte?

¿Es aquello Orión?

Se ve al revés en el hemisferio sur/norte.

Earth	La Tierra
Milky Way	La Vía Láctea
Ursa Major; The Great Bear; The Big Dipper	La Osa Mayor
The Little Bear	La Osa Menor
The Plough	El Carro
astronaut	una/un astronauta
astronomer	una/un astrónoma/o
atmosphere	la atmósfera
comet	el cometa
full moon	la luna llena
galaxy	la galaxia
meteor	el meteorito
moon	la luna
nebula	la nebulosa
planet	un planeta
shuttle	el trasbordador espacial
sky	el cielo
space	el espacio
space exploration	la exploración espacial
stars	las estrellas
sun	el sol
telescope	el telescopio
universe	el universo

INTERESTS

The Unexplained

Do you believe there's life out there?	¿Cree que hay vida fuera de la tierra?
Have you ever seen one?	¿Lo ha visto alguna vez?
Are there haunted places in (Limón)?	¿Hay lugares embrujados en (Limón)?

Lo inexplicable

DID YOU KNOW ... el cometa is a 'comet'
la cometa means 'kite'

INTERESTS

Do you believe in ...?	¿Cree en ...?
(black) magic	la magia (negra)
extraterrestrials	los extraterrestres
ghosts	fantasmas
life after death	la vida después de la muerte
mediums	las/los médiums
miracles	los milagros
telepathy	la telepatía
UFOs	los OVNIs (objetos volantes no identificados)
	(lit: objects flying not identified)
witchcraft	la brujería

ASUNTOS SOCIALES

SOCIAL ISSUES

POLITICS

LA POLÍTICA

Politics play a large part in daily Latin American life and are the topic of much conversation. Due to the greater degree of political stability in Costa Rica, the nation isn't as politically charged as most of its neighbours. Remember to always be cautious and tactful when entering a political discussion in any foreign country.

Did you hear about ...?	¿Ha oído que ...?
I read in (*La Nación*) today that ...	Hoy he leído en (*La Nación*) que ...
What do you think of the ... government?	¿Qué le parece el ...?
current	gobierno actual
new	nuevo gobierno

I (don't) agree with their policy on ...	(No) estoy de acuerdo con su política sobre ...
drugs	drogas
the economy	la economía
education	educación
the environment	el medio ambiente
military service	el servicio militar
privatisation	la privatización
social welfare	el bienestar social
I'm ...	Estoy ... de ...
against ...	en contra
in favour of ...	a favor

SOCIAL ISSUES

I support the ... party.	Apoyo al partido ...
I'm a member of the ... party.	Soy miembro del partido ...
Christian democrat	Démocrata Cristiano
communist	comunista
conservative	conservador
green	verde
social democratic	socialdemócrata
socialist	socialista
Who do you vote for?	¿Por quién vota?
I'm an anarchist.	Soy anarquista.
I'm an abstainer.	Yo me abstengo; Yo dejo en blanco.
In my country we have a (socialist) government.	En mi país tenemos un gobierno (socialista).
Politicians are all the same.	Todos los políticos son iguales.
candidate's speech	discurso
corrupt	corrupta/o
democracy	democracia
electorate	electorado
exploitation	explotación
legislation	legislación
legalisation	legalización
parliament	parlamento
party politics	los partidos políticos
policy	política
political speech	un discurso politico
polls	sondeos de opinión/encuestas
president	presidenta/e
prime minister	primer(a) ministra/o
vote	votar
... elections	elecciones ...
local council	municipales
regional	estatales/regionales
national	generales

ENVIRONMENT

Does (Puntarenas) have a
  pollution problem?

Does (San José) have a
  recycling program?

Is this recyclable?

Are there any protected
  ... here?

Is this a protected ...?
  forest
  park
  species

Where do you stand on ...?
  deforestation
  nuclear testing
  pollution

antinuclear group
biodegradable
conservation
disposable
drought
ecosystem
endangered species

hunting
industrial pollution
nuclear energy
ozone layer
recyclable
recycling
toxic waste
water supply

EL AMBIENTE

¿Hay un problema de
  contaminación en
  (Puntarenas)?

¿Hay algún programa de
  reciclaje en (San José)?

¿Esto es reciclable?

¿Hay ... protegidas/os aquí?

¿Este ... está protegida/o?
  bosque
  parque
  especie

¿Qué piensa de ...?
  la deforestación
  las pruebas nucleares
  la contaminación

el grupo antinuclear
biodegradable
la conservación
desechable
la sequía
el ecosistema
las especies en peligro de
  extinción
la caza
la contaminación industrial
la energía nuclear
la capa de ozono
reciclable
reciclar
los residuos tóxicos
el suministro de agua

SOCIAL ISSUES

THEY MAY SAY

¡Anda ya!	In your dreams!
¡Claro!	Clearly!; Of course!
¡De veras!	You don't say!
¡Eso no es verdad!	That's not true!
¡Estoy de acuerdo!	I agree!
¡Exactamente!	Exactly!
Lo que sea.	Whatever.
¡Ni hablar!/¡Para nada!	No way!
¡No estoy de acuerdo!	I disagree!
¡Por supuesto!	Absolutely!
¡Sí hombre!	Yeah, sure!

SOCIAL ISSUES

How do people feel about ...?
What do you think about ...?

I'm in favour of ...
I'm against ...
  abortion
  animal rights
  euthanasia

What's the current policy on (immigration)?
Is there an (unemployment) problem here?
Is there an adequate social welfare program?

What assistance is there for (the) ...?
  aged
  homeless
  street kids

ASUNTOS SOCIALES

¿Qué piensa la gente de ...?
¿Qué piensas de ...?

Estoy a favor de ...
Estoy en contra de ...
  el aborto
  los derechos de los animales
  la eutanasia

¿Cuál es la política actual sobre (inmigración)?
¿Existe un problema de (desempleo) aquí?
¿Hay un buen programa del bienestar social?

¿Qué tipo de asistencia reciben los ...?
  ancianos
  sin casas; callejeros (col)
  jóvenes callejeros

SOCIAL ISSUES

activist	un(a) activista
class system	el sistema de clases
demonstration	una manifestación
human rights	los derechos humanos
inequality	la desigualdad
protest	una protesta
rally	concentración
social security	la seguridad social
social welfare	el bienestar social
trade union	sindicatos
unemployment	el desempleo

SOCIAL ISSUES

DRUGS   DROGAS

Recreational drugs are illegal in Costa Rica, including marijuana
which is often used openly. If you find yourself in a position where
drugs are being discussed, the following phrases may help you
understand the conversation. If referring to your own interests,
use discretion.

I don't take drugs.	No consumo ningún tipo de drogas.
I'm not interested in drugs.	No me interesan las drogas.
I take (cocaine) occasionally.	Tomo (cocaína) de vez en cuando.

DOPE – COLLOQUIAL TERMS

One problem with being in another country is that it's often difficult to assess situations and people as easily as you can back
home, especially when you're unfamiliar with the language. Here
are some colloquial terms common among drug-users – if you
hear them in use around you, you're probably in the wrong bar.

enrular un porro	to roll a joint	jaco	heroin
caballo	heroin	mota	marijuana
chocolate	hash	pepa	LSD
chuta	syringe	perico	cocaine
coca	cocaine	yonki	heroin addict

I smoke regularly.	Fumo regularmente.
Do you want to smoke a joint?	¿Quiere fumar un porro?
I'm a heroin addict.	Soy un adicto a la heroina.
Do you sell syringes?	¿Vende jeringas?
I'm stoned.	Estoy pijiado/tostado.
I'm out of it.	Me siento un zombie.
I'm trying to get off it.	Estoy intentando dejarlo.

acid	LSD/ácidos
addiction	la adicción
cocaine	la cocaína
cold turkey	el síndrome de abstinencia
drug addiction	una drogadicción
drug dealer	un vendedor de drogas
drug trafficker	un narcotraficante
heroin addict	un(a) adicta/o a la heroina
to inject	inyectarse
overdose	una sobredosis
syringe	una jeringa

IR DE COMPRAS   SHOPPING

The **Mercado Central**, 'Central Market' in San José offers a range of goods from seafood, spices and exotic flowers to tasty, quick meals, so it's worth venturing past the souvenirs and searching the market's depths.

Don't miss the farmer's market which is held on weekends on the street outside the **Mercado Central**. Fresh Costa Rican coffee is always a good buy and makes a great present for anyone who can handle large doses of caffeine.

Otherwise, shopping depends on local artisans and specialities. Outdoor markets with local products are always a good choice for unique items such as wood and stone carvings of animals. Remember that buying turtle products, even small earrings or bracelets made from their shell, contributes to the destruction of this precious species.

LOOKING FOR ...   BUSCANDO ...

Where can I buy ...?   ¿Dónde puedo comprar ...?

Where's the nearest ...?   ¿Dónde está ... más cercana/o?

camera shop	la tienda de fotografía
clothing store	la tienda de ropa
craft shop	la tienda de artesanía
department store	los grandes almacenes; un mall
fish shop	la pescadería
general store	el almacén; la pulpería
greengrocer	la verdulería/frutería
launderette	la lavandería
market	el mercado
optician	la óptica
pharmacy	la farmácia
record shop	la tienda de casetes
shoe shop	la zapatería

shop — el almacén; la pulpería
souvenir shop — la tienda de recuerdos
stationers — la papelería
supermarket — el supermercado
tailor — la sastrería
travel agency — la agencia de viajes

MAKING A PURCHASE — COMPRANDO

I'm just looking. — Sólo estoy mirando.
How much is this? — ¿Cuánto cuesta/vale esto?
Can you write down the price? — ¿Puede escribir el precio?
I'd like to buy ... — Quisiera comprar ...
Do you have others? — ¿Tiene otros?
I don't like it. — No me gusta.
I'll buy it. — Lo compro.
Do you accept credit cards? — ¿Aceptan tarjetas de crédito?
Can I have a receipt? — ¿Podría darme un recibo?
Does it have a guarantee? — ¿Tiene garantía?
I'd like to return this please. — Me gustaría devolver esto, por favor.

It's faulty. — Es defectuosa/o.
It's broken. — Está quebrada/o.
I'd like my money back. — Quiero que me devuelvan el dinero.

THEY MAY SAY

¿En qué le puedo servir? — Can I help you?
¿Qué desea? — Can I help you?
Lo siento, es el único que tenemos. — Sorry, this is the only one.
¿Cuánto/s quiere? — How much/many would you like?
¿Algo más? — Will that be all?
¿Se lo envuelvo? — Would you like it wrapped?

SHOPPING

BARGAINING

Do you have something
    cheaper?
Could you lower the price?

I'll give you (80) colones.
No more than (50).

DISCUTIENDO EL PRECIO

¿Tiene algo más barata/o?

¿Podría bajar un poco el
    precio?
Le doy (ochenta) colones.
No más de (cincuenta).

AMOUNTS

Give me a ...
    gram
    kilogram
    millimeter
    centimeter
    meter
    half a liter

CANTIDADES

Deme ...
    un gramo
    un quilo
    un milímetro
    un centímetro
    un metro
    medio litro

SOUVENIRS

embroidery
earrings
handicrafts
jewellery
leathergoods
necklace
panama hat
pottery
ring
rug
silverware
T-shirt

RECUERDOS

bordado
pendientes/aretes
la artesanía
la joyería
los artículos de cuero
el collar; la cadena
el sombrero de panamá
la alfarería/cerámica
el anillo
la alfombra; el tapete
tenerdores y cubiertos
una camiseta/playera

SHOPPING

ESSENTIAL GROCERIES	VIVERES
Where can I find the ...?	¿Dónde puedo encontrar ...?
I'd like a/some ...	Quisiera ...
batteries	pilas/baterías
bread	pan
butter	mantequilla
cheese	queso
chocolate	chocolate
eggs	huevos
flour	harina
gas cylinder	cilindro de gas
ham	jamón
honey	miel
jam	jalea
margarine	margarina
marmalade	mermelada
matches	fósforos/cerillos
milk	leche
... olives	aceitunas ...
black	negras
green	verdes
stuffed	rellenas
olive oil	aceite de oliva
pepper	pimienta
salt	sal
shampoo	champú
soap	jabón
sugar	azúcar
sunflower oil	aceite de girasol
toilet paper	papel higiénico
toothpaste	pasta de dientes
washing powder	jabón de lavar
yogurt	yogur

SHOPPING

DID YOU KNOW ...

Contestar means to answer
Asistir means to assist

CLOTHING

	ROPA
clothing	la ropa
boots	las botas
coat	un abrigo
dress	un vestido
hat	un sombrero
jacket	una chaqueta
jeans	jeans
raincoat	un abrigo (para la lluvia)
sandals	las sandalias; las chancletas/ chanclas (col)
shirt	una camisa
shoes	los zapatos
skirt	una falda
socks	los calcetines; las medias
sweater (jumper)	suéter
swimsuit	un bañador; traje de baño
trousers	el pantalon
underwear	la ropa interior

Can I try it on?	¿Me la/lo puedo probar?
My size is ...	Uso la talla ...
It doesn't fit.	No me queda bien.

It's too ...	Es ...
big	demasiado grande; grandísima/o (col)
small	demasiado pequeña/o; pequeñísima/o (col)
short	muy corta/o; cortísima/o (col)
long	muy larga/o; larguísima/o (col)
tight	muy apretada/o; apretadísima/o (col)
loose	demasiado suelta/o; sueltísima/o (col)

SHOPPING

MATERIALS

bronze
copper
cotton
glass
leather
of brass
of gold
of silver
plastic
silk
stainless steel
wood
wool

MATERIALES

el bronce
el cobre
el algodón
el vidrio
el cuero
de latón
de oro
de plata
el plástico
la seda
el acero inoxidable
la madera
la lana

COLOURS

dark ...
light ...
black
blue
brown
green
grey
orange
pink
red
white
yellow

COLORES

... oscura/o
... clara/o
negra/o
azul
café
verde
gris
anaranjada/o
rosa
roja/o
blanca/o
amarilla/o

TOILETRIES

	COSAS PARA EL BAÑO
aftershave	la loción para después de afeitarse
comb	el peine
condoms	los preservativos/condones
dental floss	el hilo dental; la seda dental
deodorant	el desodorante
hairbrush	el cepillo (para el cabello)
moisturising cream	la crema hidratante
panty liner	una salavdora
pregnancy test kit	la prueba de embarazo
razor	la afeitadora
razor blades	las hojas de afeitar
sanitary napkins	toallas femeninas
shaving foam	la crema de afeitar
scissors	las tijeras
sunblock cream	la bronceadora
tampons	los tampones
tissues	los pañuelos de papel
toothbrush	el cepillo de dientes
water purification tablets	las pastillas para purificar el agua

(See also 'At the Chemist', page 165 and 'Essential Groceries, page 108.)

FOR THE BABY

	PARA EL BEBÉ
baby food	la comida de bebé
baby powder	el talco
bib	el babero
diaper/nappy	el pañal
disposable diapers	los pañales
feeding bottle	el biberón
diaper rash cream	la crema para la irritación de los pañales
pacifier/dummy	el chupete
powdered milk	la leche en polvo
teat (nipple)	la teta

STATIONERY & PUBLICATIONS

PAPEL Y PUBLICACIONES

Tico Times is Costa Rica's local English-language paper.

Is there an English-language bookshop nearby?

¿Hay alguna librería que venda libros en inglés por aquí cerca?

Do you have a copy of ...?

¿Tienen el libro ...?

Do you know if this author is translated into English?

¿Sabe si esta/e escritor(a) está traducida/o al inglés?

dictionary	un diccionario
envelope	un sobre
(English-language) newspaper	un periódico (en inglés)
... map	un mapa de ...
city	la ciudad
regional	la zona
road	carreteras
paper	el papel
pen	el lapicero; la pluma
popular magazines	las revistas populares

MUSIC

MÚSICA

I'm looking for a (salsa) CD.

Quisiera un compact (CD) de (salsa).

Do you have any (mambo) records?

¿Tienen discos de (mambo)?

What's her/his best recording?

¿Cuál es su mejor disco (CD)?

What's the latest record by ...?

¿Cuál es el último disco de ...?

Can I listen to this CD here?

¿Puedo escuchar este compact (CD) aquí?

Do you have this on ...?	¿Tienen este en ...?
cassette	casete
CD	compact; disco compacto
record	disco

PHOTOGRAPHY

How much is it to process this film?	¿Cuánto cuesta revelar este rollo?
When will it be ready?	¿Cuándo estará listo?
I'd like a film for this camera.	Quiero un rollo para esta cámara.
Do you have one-hour processing?	¿Tienen servicio de revelado en una hora?
I'd like to have some passport photos taken.	Me gustaría hacerme fotos de pasaporte.
This camera doesn't work.	Esta cámara no funciona.
Can you repair it?	¿Pueden arreglarla?

FOTOGRAFÍA

B&W film	película en blanco y negro
camera	la cámara (fotográfica)
color film	película en color
film	el rollo
film speed	la sensibilidad
flash	el flash
lens	el lente
slides	las diapositivas
video tape	la cinta de vídeo

SMOKING

A packet of cigarettes, please.

FUMANDO

Un paquete de cigarrillos, por favor.

Do you have a light?	¿Tiene fuego?
Do you (inf) mind if I smoke?	¿Te molesta si fumo?
Please don't smoke here.	No fume aquí por favor.
Would you like one?	¿Quiere uno?
Could I have one?	¿Me da uno?
I'm trying to give up.	Estoy intentando dejar de fumar.
cigarettes	los cigarrillos/cigarros/blancos

SHOPPING

cigarette ...	
carton	cartón de cigarros
machine	máquina de tabaco
papers	papel de fumar

cigars	los puros
filtered	con filtro
lighter	el encendedor
matches	los fósforos/cerillos
menthols	mentolados
pipe	la pipa
tobacco (for a pipe)	el tabaco de pipa
rolling tobacco	el tabaco de enrollar
without filter	sin filtro

SIZES & COMPARISONS   TAMAÑO Y COMPARACIONES

Costa Ricans are known for adding the diminutive endings -ito, -tito, -ico and -tico to words to emphasize smallness or cuteness (see Grammar page 14). It's not unusual to hear someone describing something very small as chiquitico (from chico) or even chiquitiquitico. It's this tendency to use diminutives that gives Costa Ricans the nickname Ticos.

small	chica/o; pequeña/o
big	grande
as big as	tan grande como
more	más
less	menos
some	algunas/os
also	también
neither	tampoco
enough	bastante/suficiente
a little bit	un poco/poquito/pedazo
a lot	mucho

SHOPPING

COMIDA   FOOD

One of the greatest pleasures of traveling in Costa Rica is sampling
the huge variety of fresh fruits and the tasty traditional meals (see
Comida Típica, page 121). Costa Rican cuisine is based around
rice and black beans, and is usually both fresh and healthy. Even
the smallest towns have restaurants and/or cafés (**sodas**). In San
José, you'll also find the inevitable fast-food outlets.

beakfast	desayuno
lunch	almuerzo/comida
snack	merienda
dinner	cena

VEGETARIAN &   VEGETARIANO Y
SPECIAL MEALS   COMIDA ESPECIAL

Vegetarians should have little trouble finding dishes without meat
on the menu, or can ask for a combination plate (**casado**) without the meat. The black beans served with nearly every meal
offer a good, low-fat alternative source of protein.

I'm a vegetarian.	Soy vegetariana/o.
I don't eat meat.	No como carne.
Do you have any vegetarian dishes?	¿Tienen algún plato vegetariano?
Does this dish have meat?	¿Tiene carne este plato?
Can I get this without the meat?	¿Me puede preparar este plato sin carne?
Does it contain eggs/dairy products?	¿Tiene huevos/productos lácteos?
I'm allergic to (peanuts).	Soy alérgica/o a (el maní).
Is this kosher?	¿Es apto/bueno para los judíos?
Is this organic?	¿Es orgánico?

FOOD

EATING OUT   COMIENDO EN RESTAURANTES

Many restaurants in Costa Rica have identical menus. There are **sodas**, or cafés, that serve coffee, soft drinks, snacks and often a single fixed-price dish. Otherwise, depending on location, a restaurant may focus more on seafood or chicken and beef, but are still quite similar.

San José has some variety, including Chinese and a few vegetarian restaurants. Quepos, Jaco and Tamarindo have some US, Italian and other international fare for travellers, while food in Limón province is spicier and has more of a caribbean influence.

Table for ..., please.	Una mesa para ..., por favor.
Can I see the menu please?	¿Puedo ver la carta, por favor?
Do you have a menu in English?	¿Tiene una carta en inglés?
What's that?	¿Qué es esto?
I'd like ...	Quisiera ...
Is service included in the check?	¿Está incluido el servicio en la cuenta?
Does it come with salad?	¿Viene con ensalada?
What's the soup of the day?	¿Cuál es la sopa del día?
What's the speciality here?	¿Cuál es la especialidad de este restaurante?
What do you recommend?	¿Qué me recomiende usted?
What's in this dish?	¿Qué ingredientes tiene este plato?
Do you have sauce?	¿Tiene salsa?
Not too spicy please.	No tan/muy picante, por favor.
It's not hot.	No está caliente.
I didn't order this.	No pedí esto.
I'd like something to drink.	Quiero algo para beber.
Can you please bring me (more) ...?	¿Me puede traer (mas) ..., por favor?
The check, please.	La cuenta, por favor.
Thank you, that was delicious.	Muchas gracias, la comida está muy rica.

FOOD

ashtray	cenicero
the check (bill)	cuenta
cup	taza
fork	tenedor
glass	un vaso
knife	un cuchillo
plate	un plato
restaurant	restaurante
spicy	picante
spoon	cuchara
teaspoon	cucharita
toothpick	palillo de dientes
wineglass	una copa

Condiments

chilli	chile
chilli sauce	salsa picante
garlic	ajo
mayonnaise	mayonesa
mustard	mostaza
vinegar	vinagre

Condimentos

Desserts & Snacks

appetiser in sauce	coctel
crème caramel; egg custard	flan
ice cream	helado
rice pudding	arroz con leche
sandwich	emparedado/gallo/ sandwich
soup	sopa/consomé/locro

Postres y meriendas

FOOD

MENU DECODER

a la plancha	grilled
aceitunas (rellenas)	(stuffed) olives
adobo	battered
ahumada/o	smoked
(al) ajillo	(in) garlic
ajo	garlic
al horno	baked
albóndigas	meatballs
allioli	garlic sauce
almejas	clams
anchoas	anchovies
anguila	eel
anís	anise
apanado	battered
arroz (con leche)	rice (pudding)
asada/o la parilla	grilled
asado	roasted
bien asado	well done
bacalao	salted cod
beicon con queso	cold bacon with cheese
bistec	steak
bistec con papas	steak & chips
blanco	white (wine)
bollos	bread rolls
calamares	calamari/ squid
calamares a la romana	squid rings fried in butter
caldereta	stew
caldo	broth/stock/ consommé

camarón	shrimp; small prawn
canelones	cannelloni
cangrejo de río	crayfish
carbón/al carbón	chargrilled
carne	meat
cazuela	casserole
cerdo	pork/pig
cochinillo	suckling pig
cocida/o	boiled
cocina	kitchen
coco	coconut (dried brown part)
coctél	cocktail
conejo	rabbit
cordero	lamb
costillas	ribs
crudo	raw
cuajada	milk junket with honey
la cuenta	the check (bill)
culantro	cilantro/ coriander
champiñones (al ajillo)	(garlic) mushrooms
chipirón	small squid
chivo	baby goat
chorizo	spicy red/white sausage
chuleta	chop/cutlet
dulce	sweet
empanada	meat pastry
ensalada (rusa)	salad (with mayonnaise)

FOOD

MENU DECODER

entremeses	hors-d'oeuvres	revueltos	scrambled
espagueti	spaghetti	jamón (dulce)	(boiled) ham
estofada/o	braised	una jarra	jug
estofado	stew	jengibre	ginger
faba	type of dried bean	jugo	juice
filete	fillet	langosta	spiny lobster
flan	crème caramel	langostino	large prawn
fresca/o	fresh	lechuga	lettuce
frijoles	beans	legumbre	pulse
frita/o	fried	lengua	tongue
fruta	fruit	una litrona	a liter bottle
fuerte	strong	lomo	filet
gazpacho	cold tomato and vegetable soup	macarrones	macaroni
		marinada/o	marinated
		marisco	shellfish
grasa	fat	una mediana	bottle (1/3 liter)
guiso	stew	medio crudo	rare
hamburguesa	hamburger	mejillones (al vapor)	(steamed) mussels
harina	flour		
helado	ice cream	menta	mint
hervida/o	boiled	menú del día	set menu
hierbabuena	mint	miel	honey
bien cocido	well done	milanesa (de carne)	schnitzel (pounded, breaded and fried meat)
hongos	mushrooms (and all other types of fungus)		
horneado	baked	nata	cream
horno	oven	natilla	sour cream
al horno	baked	natillas	creamy milk dessert
huevos	eggs		
cocidos duros	hard-boiled	papas fritas	French fries (chips)
fritos	fried		

FOOD

MENU DECODER

pastel	pastry/cake	ración	snack
pavía	battered	rellena/o	stuffed
pechuga	chicken breast	salado	salted/salty
pescado	fish	una sangría	sangria (red wine punch)
pescado frito	tiny fried fish		
picadillo de ...	minced ...	seco	dry/dried
picante	spicy	segundo plato	second/main course
pipa	raw, green coconut		
		soja	soy
(a la) plancha	grill(ed); served on a hot plate	sopa	soup
		tapa	bite-sized snack
un plato	a plate	tarta	cake
poco cocido	rare	termino medio	medium
postre	dessert	tocino con queso	cold bacon with cheese
potaje	stew		
primer plato	first course	tortilla	omelette
pulpo (a la gallega)	octopus (in sauce)	tortilla española; de papas	potato omelette
queque	cake	tostada	toast
queso	cheese	(carne de) vaca	beef
rabo	tail	vegetales	vegetables
		verdura	green vegetable

WILL YOU HAVE LARD WITH THAT?

Manteca, a word often used for butter in other Spanish-speaking countries, means 'lard' in Costa Rica. So be careful what you ask to have put on your toast!

TYPICAL MEALS   COMIDA TÍPICA

Costa Rican food isn't spicy, but hot chilli sauce is provided in most restaurants and homes. Meals are generally filling and healthy.

Rice and beans are almost always the centerpiece of a meal, while meat is served as just one component, rather than the central part of a dish. While there's an amazing selection of fresh fruit and vegetables, be cautious with unwashed or unpeeled fruits and vegetables. Traditional Costa Rican dishes, and regional foods include:

arroz con (pollo, camarones, etc)
achiote-flavored rice fried with onions, cilantro (coriander), carrots, peas and a choice of chicken, shrimp or a variety of other ingredients. Usually served very hot.

arroz con frijoles
white rice with black beans, sometimes served with plaintain. Eaten at breakfast, lunch or dinner.

bocas
side dishes often served with drinks at bars. These include black beans, ceviche, chicken stew, French fries, variations of taco or pieces of beef.

casado
a set, filling, and reasonably priced meal, available at most restaurants for lunch or dinner. A casado contains rice, black beans, fried plaintains, chopped cabbage, tomato and usually a choice of beef, chicken or fish. Often an egg, lime, or an avocado are included. A casado without meat, sin carne, makes a decent vegetarian dish that's available in most restaurants.

ceviche
an essential experience for anyone traveling in Costa Rica – raw fish and other seafood that's been marinated in lemon or lime, chilli, onions, garlic, tomatoes and sometimes coriander. The citric acid from the lemon or lime cooks the fish. It's served cold, often as an appetiser.

FOOD

FOOD

TYPICAL MEALS   COMIDA TÍPICA

choriadas
> fried pancakes made of fresh corn mash. They're more often served at home than in restaurants. Best hot off the grill.

elote
> corn served boiled, cocinado, or roasted on the cob, asado

empanadas
> a meat or cheese pasty that can be either fried, frita, or baked, al horno. In Costa Rica, they're usually fried.

frijoles
> beans, boiled, fried and refried and served in soups or tortillas (or with just about anything)

guacamole
> salad of mashed avocados mixed with onion, chilli, lemon and tomatoes

gallo pinto
> (lit: spotted rooster) the fried version of beans and rice often accompanied by a little fried onion, natilla (a heavy sour cream) and huevos revueltos/fritos (scrambled/fried eggs) on the side. A popular and filling breakfast choice.

gallos
> tortilla sandwiches made with meat, beans and either lettuce and tomato or cheese

olla de carne
> beef and vegetable soup made with potatoes, plaintains, corn, squash and a local tuber called yuca

palmitos
> hearts of palm – the edible inner portion of the stem of the Pejibaye palm – served in a salad with a vinegar dressing. Somewhat of a delicacy.

patacones
> coastal speciality, especially along the Caribbean, consisting of slices of deep fried plaintain

TYPICAL MEALS   COMIDA TÍPICA

FOOD

pejibaye
: a starchy palm fruit eaten in salad or with mayonnaise

picadillo
: meaning minced, there are a variety of ingredients that can come in a picadillo dish, including cooked green papaya

Salsa Lizano
: The 'secret sauce' of Costa Rica. Added to everything, especially gallo pinto (see page 122), many visitors are tempted to bring home large quantities of this tangy, yet sweet concoction.

tacos
: Costa Rican-style tacos are deep-fried and served with shredded cabbage, mayonnaise and ketchup

tamales
: corn dough left plain or stuffed with meat, beans or chillis, usually wrapped in banana leaves and sometimes in corn husks, and then steamed. A popular dish during festivities and at Christmas.

tortillas
: thin, round patties of pressed corn dough cooked on a stovetop or in a pan. In Costa Rica, omelettes are also sometimes called tortillas. If you're in the city, wheat tortillas are also available.

Desserts

arroz con leche
: milky and sweet rice pudding with a sprinking of cinnamon

flan
: a cold caramel custard

tres leches
: a moist cake prepared with cream, condensed and evaporated milk

FOOD

SELF-CATERING
In the Delicatessen

How much is (a kilo of cheese)?

Do you have anything cheaper?

What's the local speciality?

Give me (half) a kilo, please.

I'd like (six slices of ham).

Making Your Own Meals

Where can I find the ...?

I'd like some ...

(See Shopping, page 108, for some essential groceries.)

COCINANDO PARA SÍ MISMO
En la fiambrería

¿Cuánto vale/cuesta (un quilo de queso)?

¿Tiene algo más barato?

¿Cuál es la especialidad de la zona?

Deme (medio) quilo, por favor.

Deme (seis trozas de jamón).

Cocinando sus propias comidas

¿Dónde puedo encontrar ...?

Quisiera un poco de ...

WHERE IS THE ...?	
baker	panadería
butcher	carnicería
cake shop	pastelería
fish shop	pescadería
greengrocer	verdulería/frutería

AT THE MARKET
Meat & Poultry

bacon

beef

chicken

duck

goat

ham

hamburger

hot dog

EN EL MERCADO
Carnes y aves de corral

tocino

carne de res

pollo

pato

cabra/cabrito/chivo

jamón

hamburguesa

perro caliente

FOOD

kidney	riñón
lamb	cordero
liver	hígado
(minced) meat	carne (picada)
mutton	(carne de) cordero
pigeon	paloma
pork	cerdo/chancho
rabbit	conejo
roast meat	carne asada; churrasco
sausage	salchicha/chorizo
steak	bistec
tripe	mondongo
turkey	pavo
veal	ternera

Cuts — Trozos

beefsteak	bistec/bife
breast (poultry)	pechuga
chop	chuleta
fat	grasa
ribs	costillas
tongue	lengua

Fish & Seafood — Pescado y mariscos

bass	corvina
catfish	bagre
clams	almejas
crab	cangrejo
flounder (bottom fish)	pez hoja
lobster	langosta
mackerel	macarela
monkfish	rape
mussels	mejillones
octopus	pulpo
oyster	ostra
perch	mojarra

FOOD

prawns	camarones
salmon	salmón
sardine	sardina
scallop	vieira
sea bass	dorado
seafood	mariscos
shark	tiburón
shellfish	concha
shrimps	camarones
snails	caracoles
snapper	pargo
squid	calamares
swordfish	pez espada
trout	trucha
tuna	atún

Vegetables   Vegetales

artichoke	alcachofa
asparagus	espárragos
eggplant	berenjena
avocado	aguacate
beetroot	remolacha
broccoli	brócoli
Brussels sprouts	coles de bruselas repollo
cabbage	repollo
capsicum	pimentón/pimiento
carrot	zanahoria
cauliflower	coliflor
celery	apio
corn	maíz
corn on the cob	elote
cucumber	pepino
garlic	ajo
green beans	ejotes
leek	puerro
lettuce	lechuga

mushroom	hongos/champiñones
onion	cebolla
peas	guisantes
plantain (savory banana-like fruit that's cooked and often served with main dishes)	plátano
potato	papa/patata
pumpkin	calabaza
red chilli pepper	ají
spinach	espinaca
squash	calabaza/zapallito/ayote
sweet potato	batata
tomato	tomate
zucchini	calabacín

FOOD

Fruit & Nuts — Frutos y nueces

almond	almendra
apple	manzana
apricot	damasco/albaricoque
avocado	aguacate
banana	plátano dulce; banana
blackberry	mora
cherry	cereza
coconut	coco
custard apple	chirimoya
date	dátil
fig	higo
grape	uva
grapefruit	toronja
guava	guayaba
hazelnut	avellana
lemon	limón
lime	lima
mandarin	mandarina
mango	mango
melon	melón

FOOD

orange	naranja
papaya	papaya
passionfruit	maracuyá/parchita
peach	durazno/melocotón
peanut	maní/cacahuate
pear	pera
pineapple	piña
pine nut	piñón
pistachio	pistacho/e
plum	ciruela
pomegranate	granada
quince	membrillo
raspberry	frambuesa
star fruit	carambola
strawberry	fresa/frutilla
tamarind	tamarindo
watermelon	sandía

Pulses   Legumbres

beans	fríjoles
red beans	frijoles; porotos colorados
broad bean	haba
chickpea	garbanzo
kidney beans	alubias
lentils	lentejas

Breads & Cereals   Panes y cereales

cake	queque/pastel/torta
cookie (biscuit)	galleta/bizcocho
cracker	saltina; galleta salada
croissant	medialuna
pancake	panqueque/panqué
pastry	repostería
rice	arroz
sweet bread	pan dulce

DRINKS
Nonalcoholic Drinks

Fruit juices, bottled water and other soft drinks are readily available. Fresh fruit juices come in a variety of flavors and are an essential experience of Costa Rica. Be careful when buying fresh juices, as drinks made with unwashed fruit or contaminated water could cut your trip short.

FOOD

cold fizzy drink	gaseosa bien helada
(without) ice	(sin) hielo
... juice	jugo ...
orange	de naranja
pure	puro
watered juice	refresco natural con agua
	licuado
(mineral) water	agua (mineral)

un natural con leche; batido en leche
  similar to a fruit milkshake

pipas
  green coconuts which have a hole in the top so you can drink
  the milk with a straw – slightly bitter but refreshing

refresco natural
  frequently referred to simply as a natural, these drinks can be
  made to order con agua, 'with water' or con leche, 'with milk'.
  Flavors include mango, papaya, pineapple, strawberry, watermelon, cantaloupe, blackberry, carrot, tamarind, and star fruit,
  or a combination of flavors.

Alcoholic Drinks   **Bebidas alcoholicas**

Wine is scarce in Costa Rica, but beer is plentiful, to say the least. There are many local brands, but Pilsen and Imperial are the most popular. Guaro, the local firewater, is economical and packs a decent punch. If you're lucky you'll get to sample some of the contrabando, a hearty moonshine made in secret distilleries.

FOOD

FOOD

beer	cerveza/birra; una fría (col)
brandy	coñac
champagne	champán
martini	martini
moonshine	contrabando
rum	ron
spirit	guaro
(red/white) wine	vino (tinto/blanco)

Hot Drinks   Bebidas calientes

(black) coffee	café (negro)
instant coffee	nescafé
with/without milk	con/sin leche
with/without sugar	con/sin azúcar
(herbal) tea	té (aromático)
with lemon	con limón
hot chocolate	chocolate

Your Shout, My Shout   Te invito a un trago

What would you like?	¿Qué quieres tomar?
I'll have ...	Regaleme ...; Para mí, ...
It's on me.	Pago yo.
It's my round.	Es mi ronda.
You can get the next one.	La próxima la pagas tú.
Same again, please.	Lo mismo, por favor.

CHEERS!

¡Salud!
¡A tu/su salud!
¡Chin chin!
¡Buena suerte!
¡Por ti/ustedes/nosotros!
(lit: to you (sg)/you (pl)/us)

FOOD

One too Many?

Thanks, but I don't feel like it.
This is hitting the spot.
Where's the toilet?
I'm feeling drunk.
I want to throw up.
I'm hung over.

Un poco demasiado

Gracias, pero no quiero mas.
Me está pasando bien.
¿Dónde está el baño?
Me estoy emborachando.
Tengo ganas de vomitar.
Estoy de goma; Tengo resaca.

EN EL CAMPO

IN THE COUNTRY

The countryside in Costa Rica is a very different experience to the capital city of San José, with the pace of life generally much more relaxed. Although Costa Rica is a relatively small nation, there's a lot of geographical variety and some suprising regional differences.

CAMPING	**ACAMPAMIENTO**
camping ground	camping/campamento
campsite	lugar de acampar; campo
to camp	acampar

Is there a campsite nearby?	¿Hay algún lugar para acampar cerca?
Can I camp here?	¿Se puede acampar aquí?
Do you have any sites available?	¿Hay campo?

How much is it per ...?	¿Cuánto vale/cuesta por ...?
person	persona
tent	carpa/tienda
vehicle	vehículo

Where are the showers?	¿Dónde están las duchas?

can opener	el abrelatas
canvas	el sobretoldo
firewood	la leña
hammer	el martillo
hammock	la hamaca
mat	la esterilla
mattress (camping)	el colchoneta
mosquito net	el toldo
penknife	la navaja
rope	la cuerda

IN THE COUNTRY

| CAMPING | CAMPING GROUND |
| PROHIBIDO ACAMPAR | NO CAMPING |

sleeping bag	el saco de dormir
stove	la estufa/cocina
tent	la carpa; tienda (de acampar)
tent pegs	las estacas
flashlight (torch)	la linterna; el foco
water bottle	la botella de agua

HIKING & MOUNTAINEERING

ALPINISMO

Around 13 per cent of land in Costa Rica has been set aside for national parks, wildlife refuges, biological reserves and recreational areas. Most parks have plenty of short hikes, and there are several good options for longer distance hikes, including Parque Nacional Corcovado.

Getting Information

Buscando información

Where can I find out about hiking routes in the region?
¿Dónde hay información sobre caminos rurales de la zona?

Are there guided treks/climbs?
¿Se organizan excursiones?

I'd like to talk to someone who knows this area.
Quisiera hablar con alguien que conozca este sector.

Is the track (well) marked?
¿Está (bien) marcado el sendero?

How high is the climb?
¿Qué alto es la subida?

Which is the shortest/easiest route?
¿Cuál es el camino más corto/ fácil?

Is the path open all year?
¿Está la ruta abierta todo el año?

Is it a difficult/safe walk?
¿Es una caminata difícil/ segura?

Is it very scenic?
¿Tiene vista?

When does it get dark?
¿A qué hora oscurece?

Where can I hire mountain gear?
¿Dónde se alquila el equipo de montaña?

Where can we buy supplies?
¿Dónde podemos comprar comida?

How many hours per day will we walk?
¿Cuántas horas por día vamos a caminar?

How far is it from ... to ...?
¿Cuánto hay de ... a ...?

IN THE COUNTRY

On the Path

Where have you come from?	¿De dónde viene?
How long did it take you?	¿Cuánto ha tardado?
Does this path go to ...?	¿Este camino va a ...?
I'm lost.	Estoy perdida/o.
Where are we on this map?	¿Dónde estamos en el mapa?
Where can I spend the night?	¿Dónde puedo pasar la noche?
Can I leave some things here for a while?	¿Puedo dejar algunas cosas aquí durante un rato?
May I cross your property?	¿Puedo cruzar su propiedad?
Is the water OK to drink?	¿Se puede beber el agua?
Can we swim here?	¿Se puede nadar aquí?

En el camino

altitude	la altura
backpack	la mochila; el salveque
binoculars	los binoculares
cave	la cueva/caverna
cliff	el guindo
to climb	subir
compass	la brújula
cross-country trail	el camino
downhill	cuesta abajo
forest	el bosque
gap (narrow pass)	el pase estrecho
gloves	los guantes
guide	la/el guía
guided trek	la excursión guiada
harness	el arnés
to hike	ir de excursión
hiking boots	las botas de montaña
ledge	el saliente
lookout	el mirador
map	el mapa
mountain	la montaña
mountaineering	alpinismo
mountain hut	el refugio de montaña

mountain path	el sendero
pass	el paso
peak	la cumbre
pick	la piqueta; el pico
provisions	los víveres; las provisiones
rock	la roca
rock climbing	escalación
rope	la cuerda
to scale	trepar
signpost	un cartel indicator
steep	escarpada/o
trail	el sendero
trek	la excursión
uphill	cuesta arriba
view	la vista
to walk	caminar

IN THE COUNTRY

AT THE BEACH

EN LA PLAYA

Is it safe to swim?	¿Es seguro nadar aquí?
Are there rip tides?	¿Hay corrientes peligrosas?
What time is high/low tide?	¿A qué hora es la marea alta/baja?

bathing suit	el traje de baño
coast	la costa
rock	la roca
sand	la arena
sea	el mar
sun	el sol
shade	la sombra
sunblock	la crema solar; el bronceador
sunglasses	las gafas de sol
tide	la marea
towel	la toalla
wave	la ola

See also Aquatic Sports in Activities, page 151.

IN THE COUNTRY

GEOGRAPHICAL TERMS	TERMAS GEOGRAFICAS
bay	la bahía
beach	la playa
bridge	el puente
cape	el cabo
coral island	la isla de coral
the country	el campo
desert	el desierto
earth	la tierra
field	el campo
footpath	el camino
forest	el bosque
harbour	el puerto
hill	la colina; el cerro
hot spring	la fuente termal; las aguas (los baños) termales
island	la isla
jungle	la selva
lake	el lago

WEATHER

What's the weather like?	¿Qué tiempo hace?
The weather's fine/bad today.	Hace buen/mal tiempo hoy.

	Today	Tomorrow
cloudy	Está nublado.	Estará nublado.
cold	Hace frío.	Hará frío.
foggy	Hay niebla.	Habrá niebla.
frosty	helando.	Helará.
hot	Hace calor.	Hará calor.
raining	Llueve.	Lloverá.
sunny	Hace sol.	Hará sol.
windy	Hace viento.	Hará viento.

landslide	el derrumbe
marsh	el estero/pantano
mesa	la mesa
mountain range	la cordillera/sierra
mud brick	el adobe
national park	el parque nacional
pass	el paso
plain	la llanura; el llano
plateau	la meseta
rapids	los rápidos
river	el río
road	la carretera/ruta
spring	la fuente
stone	la piedra
stream	la quebrada
swamp	la ciénaga; el pantano
trail (mountain)	el sendero/camino
valley	el valle
vegetation	la vegetación
vineyard	el viñedo
volcano	el volcán
waterfall	la cascada/catarata; el salto

IN THE COUNTRY

FAUNA
Domestic Animals

FAUNA
Animales domesticos

bull	el toro
calf	el ternero
chicken	el pollo
cockerel	el gallito
cow	la vaca
donkey	el burro
duck	el pato
goat	la cabra
goose	el ganso
hen	la gallina
lamb	el cordero

horse	el caballo
mule	la mula
ox	el bueye
pig	el cerdo/cochino
sheep	la oveja

See also Pets, page 82.

IN THE COUNTRY

Wildlife
What's that animal/bird/
insect called?

Animales salvajes
¿Cómo se llama este animal/
pájaro/insecto?

anteater	el oso de hormigas
armadillo	el armadillo
bat	el murciélago
boar	el chancho de monte
coati	el pizote
deer	el venado/ciervo
fox	el zorro
goat	la cabra
guinea pig	el quilo
jaguar	el tigre/jaguar

... monkey	el mono ...
capuchin	cara blanca
howler	congo
spider	colorado
squirrel	tití

mouse	el ratón
ocelot	el manigordo/ocelote
opposum	el zorro pelón
panther	el jaguar; la pantera
peccary	el chancho de monte
puma	el león; la puma
rabbit	el conejo
racoon	el mapache
skunk	el zorro hediondo
sloth (two/three toed)	el perezoso (de dos/tres dedos)
tapir	la danta
tiger	el tigre
wolf	el lobo

IN THE COUNTRY

Reptiles   Reptilios

ctenosaur	el garrobo
iguana	la iguana
lizard	el lagarto
rattlesnake	el cascabel
snake	la culebra/serpiente

SEASONS

Costa Rica really only has two seasons – the dry season and the wet season. The following may be useful while speaking of your home country.

dry season	la temporada seca
wet season	la temporada lluviosa
summer	el verano
autumn	el otoño
winter	el invierno
spring	la primavera

IN THE COUNTRY

Aquatic Wildlife

caiman	el lagarto/cocodrilo/caimán
crocodile	el lagarto/cocodrilo
dolphin	el delfín
fish	el pescado/pez
frog	la rana
otter	la nutria
seal	la foca
shark	el tiburón
shellfish	los mariscos/moluscos
toad	el sapo
turtle	la tortuga
turtle (leatherback)	la baula
whale	la ballena

Animales acuáticos

Insects & Others

ant	la hormiga
bee	la abeja
butterfly	la mariposa
cockroach	la cucaracha
fly	la mosca
leech	la sanguijuela/babosa
mosquito	el zancudo/mosquito
scorpion	el alacrán/escorpión
snail	el caracol
spider	la araña
wasp	la avispa

Insectos y otros

Birds

	Aves y pájaros
bird	el pájaro
buzzard	el zopilote
cormorant	el cormorán
crane	la grulla
eagle	el águila
egret	la garceta/garcilla
flamingo	el flamenco
hawk	el gavilán
hummingbird	el colibrí
kingfisher	el martín pescador
macaw	la lapa; el papagayo
osprey	el águila pescadora
owl	el búho
parakeet	el perico
parrot	el loro
pelican	el pelícano
pigeon	la paloma
resplendent quetzal	el quetzal
seagull	la gaviota
strok	la cigüeña
toucan	el tucán
vulture	el zopilote/buitre
woodpecker	el carpintero

FLORA

	FLORA
bamboo	el bambú
cactus	el cacto/cactus
coconut palm	la palma de coco
crops	la cosecha
flower	la flor
grapevine	la vid/parra
leaf	la hoja
lemon tree	el palo de limones
market garden/orchard	la huerta
olive tree	el olivo

orange tree	el naranjo
orchid	la orquilla
palm tree	la palma
sugar cane	la caña de azúcar
vine	la vid
vine (swinging)	el bejuco del hombre
vineyard	la viña
wheat	el trigo

ACTIVIDADES ACTIVITIES

TYPES OF SPORT TIPOS DE DEPORTES

In Costa Rica, sport means soccer. After soccer, other popular sports include basketball, rodeo, motorcross, horse racing, sport fishing and surfing.

What sport do you play? ¿Qué deporte practica/juega?

I play/practise ... Practico ...

American football	el fútbol americano
athletics	el atletismo
baseball	el beisbol
basketball	el baloncesto/basquetbol
boxing	el boxeo
cricket	el críquet
cycling	el ciclismo
diving	el buceo
fencing	la esgrima
handball	el balonmano
hockey	el hockey
indoor soccer	el papifútbol/indoor
judo	el judo
pelota	la pelota vasca
rowing	el remo
rugby	el rugby
skiing	el esquí
soccer (football)	el fútbol
surfing	el surf
swimming	la natación
table tennis	ping pong
tennis	el tenis
weightlifting	el levantamiento de pesas

TALKING ABOUT SPORT

Do you like sport?	¿Le gustan los deportes?
Yes, very much.	Me encantan.
No, not at all.	No me gustan.
I prefer to watch rather than play.	Me gusta verlos pero no practicarlos.
What sport do you follow?	¿A qué deporte es aficionada/o?
I follow ...	Soy aficionada/o a ...
Can you play (rugby)?	¿Sabe jugar al (rugby)?
Would you like to go to a (basketball) game?	¿Le gustaría ir a un partido de (baloncesto)?
Where's it being held?	¿Dónde se juega?
How much are the tickets?	¿Cuánto valen las entradas?
What time does it start?	¿A qué hora empieza?
Who's playing?	¿Quién juega?
Who are you supporting?	¿Para qué equipo va?
I'm supporting ...	Voy por ...
What's the score?	¿Cómo van?

HABLANDO SOBRE LOS DEPORTES

Do you like sport?	¿Le gustan los deportes?

ACTIVITIES

What a ...!	¡Qué/Vaya ...!
goal	gol
kick	chute/tiro/patada
pass	pase
That was a really good game!	¡Qué partidazo!
What was the final score?	¿Cómo han quedado?
It was a draw.	Empate.

SOCCER   FÚTBOL

Almost every small town has a soccer field, and many people
follow club teams almost religiously. Soccer is so popular that
some newspapers focus almost exclusively on the sport, and only
squeeze in a few news articles around the edges.

Do you follow soccer?	¿Es aficionada/o al fútbol?
Who do you support?	¿De qué equipo es?
I support (La Liga).	Soy de (La Liga).
Who's at the top of the league?	¿Quién va primero en la tabla de división?
Who plays for ...?	¿Quién juega en el ...?
My favorite player is ...	Mi jugador favorito es ...
He's a great player.	Es un gran jugador
He played brilliantly in the match against (Heredia).	Jugó un partidazo contra (Heredia).

coach	entrenador/a
corner	corner
cup	la copa
fans	los aficionados
free kick	el tiro libre
foul	la falta

ACTIVITIES

THEY MAY SAY

¡Vamos!	Come on!
¡Goooooooool!	Goal!
¡Ese fue un penal clarísimo!	That was clearly a penalty!
¡Árbitro vendido!	The ref's an amateur (a sell-out)!
¡Fue una falta!	That was a foul!
¡Fuera de juego/lugar!	Offside!

¡Oh-ay oh-ay oh-ay oh-ay oh-ay Campeón, campeón!
(Common football chant)

goal	el gol
goalkeeper	portera/o; arquera/o
kick off	el saque
league	la liga
manager	el gerente
offside	fuera de juego/lugar
penalty	el penal
pick-up (informal) game	la mejenga (col)
player	la jugadora/el jugador
to play goalkeeper	atajar
to score/shoot	meter/marcar/chutar

MAJOR SOCCER TEAMS

La Liga (Alajuela)	Saprissa

KEEPING FIT

Where's the nearest ...?	¿Dónde está ... más cercana/o?
gym	el gimnasio
swimming pool	la piscina
tennis court	la cancha de tenis
What's the charge per ...?	¿Cuánto cobran por ...?
game	juego/partida
hour	hora
day	día
Can I hire (a) ...?	¿Es posible alquilar ...?
racquet	una raqueta
shoes	zapatillas/zapatos
Do I have to be a member to attend?	¿Hay que ser socia/o para entrar?
Where are the change rooms?	¿Dónde están los vestuarios?

ATLETECISMO

TENNIS

Would you like to play tennis?	¿Quiere jugar al tenis?
Is there a tennis court near here?	¿Hay alguna cancha de tenis aquí cerca?
How much is it to hire the court?	¿Cuánto vale alquilar la cancha de tenis?
Can you play at night?	¿Se puede jugar de noche?
Is there racquet and ball hire?	¿Se alquilan raquetas y pelotas?
grass court	la cancha de sacate; el césped
hard court	la cancha dura
hire	alquilar/rentar

TENIS

ACTIVITIES

line	la línea
net	la red
to play doubles	jugar dobles
racquet	la raqueta
serve	el servicio
tennis court	la cancha de tenis
tournament	el torneo

GAME, SET & MATCH

ace	ace	love	cero a cero
advantage	ventaja	match	el partido
deuce	iguales	point	el punto
fault	falta	set	el set
game	el juego		

... point	la pelota de ...
game	juego
set	set
match	partido

ACTIVITIES

CYCLING

Where does the race pass through?
Who's winning?
How many kilometers is today's race?
Where does it finish?

cyclist
leg (in race)
(yellow) jersey
hilly stage of the race
race against the clock
winner of a leg

CICLISMO

¿Por dónde pasa la carrera?
¿Quién va ganando?
¿Cuántos kilómetros tiene la etapa de hoy?
¿Dónde termina?

ciclista
etapa
camiseta (amarilla)
etapa de montaña
contra reloj
vencedor(a) de etapa

AQUATIC SPORTS

Surfing is one of the fastest growing sports in Costa Rica, and surfers come from all over the world to try the Costa Rican waves. Surfing's influence can be readily seen in popular culture, and as the sport develops, so does new Costa Rican surfing

DEPORTES ACUÁTICOS

GO FOR IT!

When contemplating whether or not to go for a wave, you might say ¡Dale!, meaning 'Go for it!'

jargon. Much of Costa Rican surfing terminology comes directly from English – a 'beachbreak' is un beachbreak, and 'a ding' is often referred to as un ding. However, you can't assume that you'll always get by only using English.

board bag	la bolsa de tabla
boardshorts	la panta; los boardshorts
boogieboard	el boguí
diving	el buceo
diving equipment	el equipo de inmersión/el buceo
fin key	la llave para los fins
leash	el leash
motorboat	la panga
riptide	la corriente peligrosa
sunscreen	creama solar; bronceador
surfboard	la tabla (de surf)
surfer	le surfo/surfeador
to surf	surfear/sorfear
surfing	el surfeo
swimming	la natación
tide	la marea
tube	el tubo
water-skiing	el esquí acuático
water-skis	los esquís para el agua
wave	la ola
wax	la cera
windsurfing	el windsurf; la tabla de vela

See also At the Beach, page 137.

ACTIVITIES

BULLFIGHTING & RODEOS

LA CORRIDA, EL TOREO & EL RODEO

Unlike in some other Latin American countries and in Spain, the killing of a bull during a bullfight is illegal in Costa Rica. The bullfighter should only stay long enough in the ring to show their skill.

Rodeos are also popular. Riders – usually after drinking a fair amount of alcohol – see how long they can stay on a bucking bull, and then collect tips from the audience. Others demonstrate their ability by taming and controlling the hostile animals.

Do you like bullfighting?	¿Le gustan los toros?
Is bullfighting popular in this area?	¿Son populares los toros en esta región?
Is there a bullfight today/soon?	¿Hay alguna corrida de toros hoy/pronto?

Where's the bullring?	¿Dónde está la plaza de toros (la corrida)?
Who's appearing tonight?	¿Quién torea esta tarde?
What's the bullfighter called?	¿Cómo se llama el torero?
What's that music?	¿Qué es esa música?
What's happening now?	¿Qué pasa ahora?

Bullfighting Terms

Términos de corridas de toros

la corrida	bullfight
los cuernos	horns
la plaza de toros	bullring
el ruedo	arena
el torero	name given to different types of bullfighters
el toro	bull
el toro bravo	fighting bull

ACTIVITIES

HORSE RIDING

MONTANDO A CABALLO

Is there a horse-riding school around here?	¿Hay alguna escuela de equitación?
How long is the ride?	¿Cuánto dura el paseo?
How much does it cost?	¿Cuánto vale/cuesta?
Do you have rides for beginners?	¿Ofrecen paseos para principiantes?
I'm an experienced rider.	Soy un(a) jinete con experiencia
Can I rent a hat and boots?	¿Se pueden alquilar el casco y las botas de montar?

MOTORCROSS & CAR RACING

a crash	un accidente
to crash/collide	chocar
driver	la/el corredor(a); la/el piloto
to fall behind	quedarse atrás; rezagarse
Formula One	Fórmula Uno
helmet	el casco
... kilometers an hour	... kilómetros por hora
lap	una vuelta
to overtake	pasar/adelantar
racetrack	el autódromo; la pista de carreras
motorbike	el moto
racing car	el coche de carreras
to skid	patinar
to take the lead	llevar la delantera

CARRERA DE MOTO Y AUTO

GOLF

bunker	el búnker
flagstick	la banderola
follow-through	el impulso
golf course	el campo de golf
golf trolley	el carrito de golf
golfball	la pelota de golf
hole	el hoyo
iron	el bastón de hierro; el iron
teeing ground	la salida; el tee
wood	el bastón de madera; un driver

GOLF

ACTIVITIES

GAMES

Do you want to play ...?
How do you play ...?
  billiards
  cards
  chess
  computer games
  draughts
  pool
  table football

I'm sorry, I don't know how to play.
What are the rules?
It's my turn.
Stop cheating!

JUEGOS

¿Jugamos a ...?
¿Cómo se juega ...?
  al billar; el pool
  a las cartas; naipe
  al ajedrez
  con juegos de computador
  a las damas
  el billar pool
  el futbolín

Lo siento, pero no sé jugar.

¿Cuáles son las reglas?
Es mi turno; Me toca a mi.
¡No hagas trampa!

CHESS

bishop	el alfil
pawn(s)	el peón(es)
pieces	las fichas
black pieces	las negras
white pieces	las blancas
castle	la torre
queen	la reina
chess board	el tablero de ajedrez
rook	el alfil
king	el rey
knight	el caballo
stalemate	tablas

ACTIVITIES

Chess Ajedrez

Shall we play chess?	¿Jugamos al ajedrez?
White starts.	Las blancas empiezan.
It's my move.	Ahora muevo yo.
Hurry up and make a move!	¡Mueve de una vez!
Check to the king!	¡Jaque al rey!
Check(mate)!	¡Jaque (mate)!
Cheat!	¡Tramposa/o!

FESTIVALES Y DÍAS FERIADAS

FESTIVALS & HOLIDAYS

BIRTHDAYS & SAINTS' DAYS

DÍAS DE CUMPLEAÑOS Y DE SANTOS

When's your birthday?	¿Cuándo es su día de cumpleaños
My birthday is on ...	Mi día de cumpleaños es el día ...
Congratulations!	¡(Muchas) felicitaciones!
Happy birthday!	¡Feliz cumpleaños!
Many happy returns!	¡Que cumplas muchos más!
Blow out the candles!	¡Sopla las velas/candelas!

CHRISTMAS & NEW YEAR

LA NAVIDAD Y EL AÑO NUEVO

Christmas begins on 24 December, but gifts aren't usually exchanged until either New Year's Day or Epiphany on 6 January.

Merry Christmas!	¡Feliz navidad!
Happy New Year!	¡Feliz/Próspero año nuevo!

Christmas Day	la Navidad	25 December
Christmas Eve	la Nochebuena	24 December
New Year's Eve	el fin de año	31 December
New Year's Day	el año nuevo	1 January
Epiphany	día de los reyes magos	6 January

Christmas Delicacies

Delicacias de la Navidad

Many types of delicious food are served during the holidays, and each family, town or region may have its own specialties. A standard Christmas delicacy is **tamales**, which consists of corn dough wrapped in a banana leaf and stuffed with beef, chicken or cheese. **Tamales** are made in large quantities so many people can join in the feast.

FESTIVALS & TRADITIONS
FESTIVALES Y TRADICIONES

Although there are many local festivals, these are some of the most celebrated.

Semana Santa
Holy Week – the week before Easter, celebrated with religious processions

Día de los Santos
All Saint's Day – a public holiday held on 1 November. In San José, a version of North American Halloween on 31 October is also becoming popular.

Día de los Reyes Magos
(lit: three wise men's day) Epiphany – this celebration includes a procession featuring the Three Wise Men and other Christmas characters, either on the night of 5 or 6 January

Los Quince Años; La Quinceañera
when a young girl turns 15, there's a special celebration to welcome her into womanhood

TOASTS & CONDOLENCES
BRINDAS Y PÉSAMES

Bon appétit!	¡Buen provecho!
Bon voyage!	¡Buen viaje!
Good luck!	¡Buena suerte!
Hope it goes well! (inf)	¡Qué te vaya bien!
Bless you! (after sneezing)	¡Salud!; ¡Jesús!
Get well soon! (inf)	¡Que te mejores!
What bad luck!	¡Qué mala suerte!
I'm very sorry.	Lo siento muchísimo.
My thoughts are with you.	Estoy pensando en ti.

LA SALUD   HEALTH

In most big cities there are well-equipped medical services where
you can go in the case of an emergency. In country areas, regional
clinics are usually the best place to seek medical advice. Ask a local
where the closest one is if you need to get there quickly.

AT THE DOCTOR

I'm sick.	Estoy enferma/o.
My friend is sick.	Mi amiga/o está enferma/o.
I need a doctor (who speaks English).	Necesito un(a) doctor(a) (que hable inglés).
Could you please call a doctor?	¿Podría llamar a un doctor, por favor?

VISITANDO EL MÉDICO

THEY MAY SAY

¿Qué le pasa?	What's the matter?
¿Le duele?	Do you feel any pain?
¿Dónde le duele?	Where does it hurt?
¿Tiene la regla?	Are you menstruating?
¿Tiene fiebre?	Do you have a temperature?
¿Cuanto tiempo que se siente así?	How long have you been like this?
¿Ha tenido esto antes?	Have you had this before?
¿Toma medicina?	Are you on medication?
¿Fuma usted?	Do you smoke?
¿Bebe usted?	Do you drink?
¿Toma drogas?	Do you take drugs?
¿Es alérgica/o a alguna medicina?	Are you allergic to anything?
¿Está embarazada?	Are you pregnant?

HEALTH

Could the doctor come here?	¿Puede visitarme aqui la/el doctor(a)?
Where's the nearest ...?	¿Dónde está ... más cercano?
chemist	la farmacia
clinic	la clínica
dentist	el dentista
doctor	el doctor/médico
hospital	el hospital

AILMENTS

ENFERMEDADES

I'm ill.	Estoy enferma/o.
I feel under the weather.	Tengo malestar general.
I feel nauseous.	Tengo náuseas; Estoy mareado.
I've been vomiting.	He estado vomitando.
I can't sleep.	No puedo dormir.
I'm on regular medication for (a/an) ...	Estoy bajo medicación para ...
I have (a/an) ...	Tengo ...
allergy	una alergia
altitude sickness	enfermo de la altura
anaemia	anemia
blister	una ampolla
bruise	un cardenal/morado/contusión
burn	una quemadura
cancer	cáncer
cystitis	la cistitis
cholera	cólera
cold	un resfriado/catarro/resfrío
constipation	estreñimiento
cough	tos
diarrhoea	diarrea

HEALTH

dysentry	disentería
earache	dolor de oído
fever	fiebre
glandular fever	mononucleosis
headache	dolor de cabeza
hayfever	alergia al paja/polen
hepatitis	hepatitis
indigestion	indigestión
infection	una infección
inflammation	una inflamación
influenza	gripe
itch	comezón/picazón
lice	piojos
lump	un bulto
migraine	migraña/jaqueca
pain	dolor
rash	una irritación/erupción/ sarpullido
sore throat	dolor de garganta
sprain	una torcedura/ tronchadura/esquince
STD	una enfermedad de transmisión sexual
stomachache	dolor de estómago
sunburn	una quemadura de sol
sunstroke	una insolación
swelling	una hinchazón
thrush	afta
travel sickness	mareo
worms	gusanos/parasitos
yellow fever	fiebre amarilla
I feel ...	Me siento ...
dizzy	mareada/o
shivery	destemplada/o; escalofrios
weak	débil

HEALTH

I feel better/worse. | Me siento mejor/peor.
This is my usual medicine. | Éste es mi medicamento normal.

I've been vaccinated. | Estoy vacunada/o.
Do you have a student/pensioner discount? | ¿Hay algún descuento para estudiantes/pensionados?
Can I have a receipt for my health insurance? | ¿Puede darme un recibo para mi seguro médico?

WOMEN'S HEALTH   LA SALUD DE MUJERES

Could I see a female doctor? | ¿Puede examinarme; revisarme una doctora?

I'm on the Pill. | Tomo la píldora.
I think I'm pregnant. | Creo que estoy embarazada.
I haven't had my period for ... weeks. | Hace ... semanas que no me viene la menstruación.
I'd like to get the morning-after pill. | Quisiera tomar la píldora del día siguiente.
I'd like to have a pregnancy test. | ¿Puede hacerme la prueba del embarazo?
I'm pregnant. | Estoy embarazada/encinta.
I'd like to use contraception. | Quisiera usar algún método anticonceptivo.

abortion | el aborto
diaphragm | el diafragma
IUD | el DIU
mamogram | la mamografía
menstruation | la regla la menstruación
miscarriage | el aborto natural
pap smear | la citología
period pain | el dolor menstrual
the Pill | la píldora
pregnant | embarazada/encinta
premenstrual tension | la tensión pre-menstrual
ultrasound | el ultrasonido

HEALTH

SPECIAL HEALTH NEEDS

I'm ...
  asthmatic
  diabetic
  epileptic

I'm allergic to ...
  antibiotics
  aspirin
  bees
  codeine
  dairy products
  penicillin
  pollen

NECESIDADES ESPECIALES DE LA SALUD

Soy ...
  asmática/o
  diabética/o
  epiléptica/o

Soy alérgica/o ...
  a los antibióticos
  a la aspirina
  a las abejas
  a la codeína
  a los productos lácteos
  a la penicilina
  al polen

I have high/low blood pressure.	Tengo la presión baja/alta.
I have a weak heart.	Tengo el corazón débil.
I'm on a special diet.	Sigo una dieta especial.
I have a skin allergy.	Tengo un alergia en la piel.
I have my own syringe.	Tengo mi propia jeringa.
I don't want a blood transfusion.	No quiero que me hagan una transfusión de sangre.
inhaler	el inhalador
pacemaker	el marcapasos

HEALTH

ALTERNATIVE TREATMENTS

aromatherapy
   la aromaterapia
herbalist
   el herborista/homeopata
homeopathy
   la homeopatía
massage
   el masaje
massage therapist
   la masajista
meditation
   la meditación
naturopath
   el naturópata; la naturista
reflexology
   la reflexología
yoga
   el yoga

TRATAMIENTO ALTERNATIVO

PARTS OF THE BODY   PARTES DEL CUERPO

In Spanish, body parts are usually referred to as 'the' not 'my' –
it's la cabeza, 'the head', not mi cabeza, 'my head'.

My ... hurts.   Me duele ...
I have a pain in my ...   Siento dolor en ...
I can't move my ...   No puedo mover ...

ankle	el tobillo	chest	el pecho
appendix	el apéndice	ear (outer)	la oreja
arm	el brazo	ear (inner)	el oído
back	la espalda	eye	el ojo
bladder	la vejiga	finger	el dedo
blood	la sangre	foot	el pie
bone	el hueso	hand	la mano
breast	el pecho	head	la cabeza

heart	el corazón	skin	la piel
jaw	la mandíbula	shoulders	los hombros
knee	la rodilla	spine	la columna
leg	la pierna		(vertebral)
liver	el hígado	stomach	el estómago
mouth	la boca	teeth	los dientes
muscle	el músculo	throat	la garganta
nose	la nariz	tongue	la lengua
penis	el pene	vagina	la vagina
ribs	las costillas	vein	la vena

HEALTH

AT THE CHEMIST   EN LA FARMACIA

In Costa Rica, many drugs are sold over the counter without a prescription. At most drugstores you can find medicines made by major pharmaceutical companies, but it's important to know exactly what you need and to check the use-by dates on any drugs you buy.

Where's the nearest all-night chemist?	¿Dónde está la farmacia de veinti-cuatro horas más cercana?
I need something for ...	Necesito algo para ...
I have a prescription.	Tengo receta médica.
How many times a day?	¿Cuántas veces al día?
Take (two) tablets (four) times a day.	Tome (dos) pastillas (cuatro) veces al día.
before/after meals	antes/después de la comidas
Could I please have ...?	¿Me dá ... por favor?
antibiotics	antibióticos
aspirin	las aspirinas
contraceptives	los anticonceptivos
cough medicine	algo para el tos
laxatives	los laxantes
painkillers	los analgésicos
sleeping pills	las pastillas para dormir
a ... vaccine	una vacuna ...

HEALTH

AT THE DENTIST
I have a toothache.

I have a cavity.
I've lost a filling.
I've broken a tooth.
My gums hurt.
I don't want it extracted.

Please give me an anaesthetic.
Ouch!

VISITANDO EL DENTISTA
Me duele un diente/una
    muela.
Tengo una caries.
Perdí un empaste.
Quebré un diente.
Me duelen las encías.
No quiero que me lo
    arranque.
Por favor, dame anestesia.
¡Ay!

NECESIDADES ESPECIFICAS

SPECIFIC NEEDS

DISABLED TRAVELERS

VIAJEROS INCAPACITADOS

Although buses aren't equiped for wheelchair access, taxis can be hired to any destination in the country, for the right price. As few hotels and restaurants have wheelchair access – apart from those which are new or recently remodelled – disabled people planning a trip to Costa Rica should call ahead of time to check facilities.

What services are available for disabled people?	¿Qué servicios tienen para minusvalidos?
I need assistance, I'm ...	Necesito asistencia, porque soy ...
blind	ciega/o
deaf	sorda/o
disabled	minusválida/o
mute	muda/o
Is there wheelchair access?	¿Hay acceso para la silla de ruedas?
Are guide dogs allowed?	¿Se permite la entrada a los perros guía?
Is there a guide service for blind people?	¿Hay algún servicio de guía para personas ciegas?
Could you please speak more slowly/clearly?	Por favor hable más despacio/claro.
I'm hard of hearing.	Tengo problemas de oír.
Speak into my other ear please.	Hábleme por el otro oído, por favor.
I wear a hearing aid.	Llevo audífono.

GAY TRAVELERS   VIAJEROS HOMOSEXUALES

Words describing sexual orientation are more or less the same in Spanish as they are in English – although with Spanish pronunciation of course. The derogatory Costa Rican term for a homosexual is **playo**. Although Costa Rica is generally a tranquil country, machismo and homophobia are strong in many places. It's advised to be very tactful when discussing sexual orientation.

SPECIFIC NEEDS

Are there any gay bars around here? — ¿Hay algún bar gay/de ambiente por aquí?

Is there a local gay publication? — ¿Conoce alguna revista de tema homosexual?

Is there a gay bookshop? — ¿Hay alguna librería homosexual?

Am I likely to be harassed for being gay? — ¿Me van a molestar por ser homosexual?

TRAVELING WITH A FAMILY   VIAJANDO CON LA FAMILIA

I'm traveling with my family. — Viajo con toda mi familia.

Are there facilities for babies? — ¿Hay facilidades para bebés?

Is there a childminding service in the hotel? — ¿Tienen guardería en el hotel?

Can you provide an (English-speaking) babysitter? — ¿Disponen de un servicio de niñeras (que hablen inglés)?

(In Costa Rica, the word 'babysitter' is also commonly used.)

Can you add an extra bed to the room? — ¿Pueden añadir una cama en la habitación?

Does this car have a child seat? — ¿Este carro tiene sillita para niños?

Is there children's entertainment here? — ¿Hay algún espectáculo para niños aquí?

Is there a family price? — ¿Hay un precio especial para familias?

Are children allowed? — ¿Se admiten niños?

Do you have a highchair for the baby?	¿Tienen una silla para el bebé?
Is there a children's menu?	¿Tienen menú infantil?
Could you make it a child's portion?	¿Puede prepararme una ración para niños?
Is there a playground around here?	¿Hay algún parque infantil cerca?

LOOKING FOR A JOB

BUSCANDO EMPLEO

I'm looking for work.	Estoy buscando trabajo.
Do you have any vacancies for a ...?	¿Hay algún puesto de trabajo para un(a) ...?
I have a qualification in ...	Estoy cualificada para ...
I have experience in ...	Tengo experiencia ...
cleaning	en trabajos de limpieza
construction work	en la construcción
fruit picking	en la recolección de fruta
childcare	en cuidar niños
office work	en trabajo de oficina
sales	como vendedor(a)
teaching	en la enseñanza
using computers	en computadoras
waiting	como camarera/o
I'm looking for ...	Estoy buscando trabajo ...
casual work	esporádico
part-time	de tiempo parcial
full-time	de tiempo completo
What's the salary?	¿Cuál es el salario?
How is the salary paid?	¿Cuanto es el salario?
Do I have to pay tax?	¿Tengo que pagar impuestos?
What are the working hours?	¿Cuál es el horario?
I'd like to apply for the position.	Me gustaría solicitar el puesto.

Here's my résumé.	Aquí está mi currículum.
I can provide references.	Puedo presentarle mis referencias.
I have a valid work permit.	Tengo permiso de trabajo.
I'll be able to work until (May).	Puedo trabajar aquí hasta (mayo).

SPECIFIC NEEDS

ON BUSINESS   DE NEGOCIOS

Here are some key words and phrases for that quick visit or conference.

I'm here on business.	Estoy de viaje de negocios.
We're attending a ... conference trade fair	Estamos asistiendo a una ... conferencia feria de muestras
Does the hotel have office facilities?	¿Dispone el hotel de servicios de oficinas?
I need an interpreter.	Necesito un(a) intérprete.
I have an appointment with ...	Tengo una cita con ...
I need to ... send a fax/email make photocopies use a computer	Tengo que ... enviar un fax/email hacer fotocopias usar un computador
Thank you for seeing me.	Gracias por atenderme.
Let me introduce my colleague.	¿Puedo presentarle a mi colega?
It was a pleasure meeting you.	Encantada/o de conocerla/lo.
We'll be in touch.	Nos mantendremos en contacto.
Here's my business card.	Aquí tiene mi tarjeta de visita.

business card	tarjeta de visita/presentación
client	clienta/e
colleague	colega
contract	contrato
director	director
manager	encargada/o; gerente
presentation	presentación
proposal	propuesta
sales (department)	(departamento de) ventas

ON TOUR

We're traveling in a group.
I'm with a band/team.

We're here for (three nights).
We've lost our equipment.

Please talk to the ...
    group leader
    guide
    manager

We sent our gear in this ...

    bus
    plane
    train

We're playing on ... night.
Would you like some tickets?

DE GIRA

Somos parte de un grupo.
Vengo con un grupo de
    música/equipo deportivo.
Nos quedaremos (tres noches).
Hemos perdido nuestras cosas.

Por favor, hable con la/el ...
    líder del grupo
    guía
    mánager

Hemos enviado nuestras
cosas en este ...
    bus
    vuelo
    tren

Tocamos el ... por la noche.
¿Quiere entradas para
    nuestro concierto?

SPECIFIC NEEDS

FILM & TV

We're on location.

We're filming here for (six) days.

Who should we ask for permission to film here?

Can we film here?

We're making a ...
  documentary
  film
  series

actor	la actriz/el actor
camera operator	la/el operador(a)
director	la/el director(a)
editor	la/el editor(a)
presenter	la/el presentador(a)
producer	la/el productor(a)
scriptwriter	la/el guionista
camera	la cámara
editing suite	control de edición
lights	las luces
make-up	el maquillaje
prop	el decorado
script	el guión
sound	el sonido
stunt	la escena peligrosa
van	la caravana
wardrobe	el vestuario

CINE Y TELEVISIÓN

Estamos rodando los exteriores.

Vamos a rodar aquí durante (seis) días.

¿A quién tenemos que pedirle permiso para rodar aquí?

¿Podemos rodar aquí?

Estamos haciendo ...
  un documental
  una película
  una serie de televisión

THEY MAY SAY

¡Acción!	Action!	¡Toma uno!	Take One!
¡Estamos rodando!	We're filming!	¡Corten!	Cut!
¡Rodando!	Rolling!		

PILGRIMAGE & RELIGION

Is there a church nearby?	¿Hay alguna iglesia aquí cerca?
Where can I ...?	¿Dónde puedo ...?
pray	rezar
worship	hacer oración
When are services held?	¿Cuándo se celebran los oficios?
When's the church/cathedral open?	¿A qué hora abre la iglesia/catedral?
Can I attend this service?	¿Puedo asistir a este oficio?

baptism	el bautizo
bible	la Biblia
candle	la vela/candela
chapel	la capilla
church	la iglesia
communion	la comunión
confession	la confesión
God	Dios
mass	la misa
mosque	la mezquita
Pope	Papa
prayer	la oración
prayer book	el devocionario; el libro de rezos/oraciónes
priest	el sacerdote
service	el oficio
shrine	la capilla/altar
synagogue	la sinagoga
temple	el templo
worship	la adoración

For religions, see page 38.

PEREGRENACIÓN Y RELIGIÓN

SPECIFIC NEEDS

SPECIFIC NEEDS

TRACING ROOTS & HISTORY

SIGUIENDO LA HISTORIA DE LA FAMILIA

My family came from this area.
Mi familia viene de esta zona.

My ancestors came from around here.
Mis antepasados vienen de esta zona.

Is there anyone here by the name of ...?
¿Hay alguien aquí que se llama ...?

Where's the cemetery?
¿Dónde está el cementerio?

TIEMPO Y FECHAS

TIME & DATES

TELLING THE TIME   LA HORA

As much of rural Costa Rica hasn't had electricity until recently, many people still follow a natural timeclock, waking at sunrise and going to bed soon after sundown.

Just as addresses are usually explained by landmarks instead of street numbers, time is often denoted as a general 'morning', 'afternoon', or 'evening' instead of stating the actual time. When traveling in Costa Rica, keep in mind that life doesn't function with the same strict punctuality that many of us are accustomed to.

What time is it?	¿Qué hora es?
It's one o'clock.	Es la una.
It's (two o'clock).	Son las (dos).
It's five past six.	Son las seis y cinco.
It's half past eight.	Son las ocho y media.
It's a quarter to four.	Son las cuatro menos cuarto;
	Son cuarto para las cuatro.
It's (about) eleven.	Son las once (más o menos).

in the early morning (dawn)	de la madrugada
in the morning (sunrise until 12 pm)	de la mañana
midday (12 pm)	mediodía
in the afternoon (1 pm until dark)	de la tarde
in the evening (dark until sunrise)	de la noche

DAYS   DÍAS

Monday	lunes	Friday	viernes
Tuesday	martes	Saturday	sábado
Wednesday	miércoles	Sunday	domingo
Thursday	jueves		

MONTHS

MESES

January	enero
February	febrero
March	marzo
April	abril
May	mayo
June	junio
July	julio
August	agosto
September	se(p)tiembre
October	octubre
November	noviembre
December	diciembre

TIME & DATES

DATES

FECHAS

Dates are expressed by cardinal numbers (such as 'two of May'), except for the first day of the month which uses the ordinal number 'first'.

What's the date today?	¿Qué día es hoy?
It's April 26.	Es el veintiséis de abril.
	(lit: it-is the 26 of April)
It's August 3.	Es el tres de agosto.
	(lit: it-is the three of August)
It's October 1.	Es el primero de octubre.
	(lit: it-is the first of October)

PRESENT

today	hoy
this morning	esta mañana/madrugada
this afternoon	esta tarde
tonight	esta noche
this week	esta semana
this month	este mes
this year	este año
now	ahora/ya
pretty soon	ahorita
right now	en este momento

PRESENTE

PAST

yesterday	ayer
day before yesterday	anteayer
yesterday morning	ayer por la mañana/madrugada
yesterday afternoon/night	ayer por la tarde/noche
last night	anoche
last week	la semana pasada
last month	el mes pasado
last year	el año pasado
(half an hour) ago	hace media hora
(three) days ago	hace (tres) días
(five) years ago	hace (cinco) años
a while ago	hace un rato
since (May)	desde (mayo)

PASADO

TIME & DATES

FUTURE

tomorrow	mañana
day after tomorrow	pasado mañana
tomorrow morning	mañana por la mañana
tomorrow afternoon	mañana por la tarde
tomorrow evening	mañana por la noche
next week	la semana que viene/entra
next month	el mes que viene/entra

FUTURO

next year	el año que viene/entra
in (five) minutes	dentro de (cinco) minutos
in (six) days	dentro de (seis) días
within an hour/month	dentro de una hora/un mes
until (June)	hasta (junio)

DURING THE DAY   ## DURANTE EL DÍA

It's early.   Es temprano.
It's late.   Es tarde.

lunchtime	hora de comer
midnight	medianoche
noon	mediodía
sunrise	amanecer
sunset	puesta del sol; atardecer

NÚMEROS Y CANTIDADES

NUMBERS & AMOUNTS

CARDINAL NUMBERS

NÚMEROS CARDINALES

0	cero	30	treinta
1	uno	31	treinta y uno
2	dos	32	treinta y dos
3	tres	40	cuarenta
4	cuatro	41	cuarenta y uno
5	cinco	50	cincuenta
6	seis	51	cincuenta y uno
7	siete	60	sesenta
8	ocho	70	setenta
9	nueve	80	ochenta
10	diez	90	noventa
11	once	100	cien
12	doce	110	ciento diez
13	trece	200	doscientos
14	catorce	300	trescientos
15	quince	400	cuatrocientos
16	dieciséis	500	quinientos
17	diecisiete	600	seiscientos
18	dieciocho	700	setecientos
19	diecinueve	800	ochocientos
20	veinte	900	novecientos
21	veintiuno	1000	mil
22	veintidós	2000	dos mil
23	veintitrés	5000	cinco mil
24	veinticuatro	2200	dos mil doscientos

one million	un millón
48	cuarenta y ocho
157	ciento cincuenta y siete
1240	mil doscientos cuarenta
14800	catorce mil ochocientos
1999	mil novecientos noventa y nueve

ORDINAL NUMBERS / NÚMEROS ORDINALES

1st	primera/o (1r)
2nd	segunda/o
3rd	tercera/o
4th	cuarta/o
5th	quinta/o
6th	sexta/o
7th	séptima/o
8th	octava/o
9th	novena/o
10th	décima/o

FRACTIONS / FRACCIONES

a quarter	un cuarto
a third	un tercio
half	media/o
three-quarters	tres cuartos

USEFUL WORDS / PALABRAS ÚTILES

Enough!	¡Basta!
a little (amount)	un poquito
double	(el) doble
a dozen	una docena
few	(unas) pocas/(unos) pocos
less	menos
many	muchas/os
more	más
a pair	un par
per cent	por ciento

LIMÓN CREOLE

Costa Rica is considered the most westernized country in Central America, due to its dominant Caucasian, Catholic, and Castillian influences. The 1989 Census classified 98 per cent of the population as 'white' or 'mestizo', and remaining two per cent as 'black' or 'indigenous'. Although Afro-Costa Ricans make up a relatively small percentage of the population, in the Caribbean province of Limón – which covers the entire Caribbean coast of Costa Rica – they constitute over a third of the population. With over 80,000 in Limón, Afro-Costa Ricans are the largest minority in the country. Anyone who visits popular Limón destinations like Puerto Limón, Puerto Viejo or Cahuita will notice striking differences in people's appearance, clothes, food, architecture, music, religion and, of course, language.

The language of the Afro-Costa Rican people is as unique as the people themselves. This idiom, often referred to as **criollo limones**, 'Limón Creole', is a mix of the various languages, cultures and other influences of the region.

Therefore, Limón Creole isn't a standardized language like English or Spanish. As this language changes from speaker to speaker, and changes even more so from generation to generation, it's impossible to write a definitive phrasebook on it. However, if you take into account the origins of Limón Creole and look at some examples of speech, you'll get a better understanding of how to approach the language.

To understand the origins of the language of Afro-Costa Rican people, you have to look back to the beginning of their inhabitance in the country. Unlike most Central American countries, the black population were not in Costa Rica because of slavery. There were fewer than 200 slaves in Costa Rica when the institution was abolished in 1824. The majority of the Afro-Costa Ricans' ancestors emigrated from the Caribbean islands, particularly from Jamaica, during the end of the 19th century in search of work and a new start. Many came as seasonal workers who never intended to stay permanently, and therefore made little attempt to learn Spanish. In many ways, English had more social status, and many English-speaking blacks looked upon the Hispanic majority in Costa Rica with disdain.

The government didn't offer citizenship to immigrants, and forbade travel for 'people of color' outside the coastal province. Subsequently, Limón developed as a nation within the borders of Costa Rica. English along with the Jamaican variation of English, Jamaican Creole, were the languages used in both business and in the home. English, including Jamaican and other West Indian dialects, as.well as local dialects were taught in schools to the younger generations.

During the 1920s, the banana plantations of Limón became successful, but there was a scarcity of work elsewhere in Costa Rica. As a result, Hispanics flooded into the region in search of employment. Little more than 10 years later, a major blight struck the banana crops and the fruit companies moved the plantations to the Pacific coast. Most blacks were now without work, and since they weren't technically citizens, many Hispanics took their land. Spanish became the more prestigious language of business and education, while Jamaican Creole had little prestige and came to have the derogatory label 'Banana Talk'.

After the Revolution of 1948 (several weeks of civil warfare during which over 2000 people were killed, and which resulted in the National Liberation Party emerging as Costa Rica's new government), citizenship was granted to Afro-Costa Ricans and their situation began to improve. As communication, travel and business increased between Limón and the rest of the country, Spanish influence in the language of Limón also increased. An example that shows the great degree of Spanish influence in Limón Creole is that many younger people cannot distinguish between the pronunciation of 'yo-yo' and 'jo-jo' – much the same as a Spanish speaking Costa Rican – as the 'zh' sound, as in 'gen-darme', has come to be pronounced as Spanish 'll/y'.

Looking at the same sentence in Standard English, Jamaican Creole, Spanish and Limón Creole can give a good indication of how sentences in Limón Creole are formed. Jamaican Creole and Limón Creole sentences are spelled phonetically to give a better idea of how they actually sound.

LIMÓN CREOLE

bar	the mouth of a river, as in Sixaola Bar
barbeque	wooden dryers used to dry cocoa and coconut meat
calabash	gourds, often hollowed out and used as containers
college	secondary school, from Spanish *colegio*
cents	used in place of *céntimos* – one hundred cents = one *colón*
deputy	local politician, from Spanish *diputado*
fresco	soft drink, from Spanish *refresco*
gibnut	a large spotted rodent that's often hunted
gig	a homemade wooden spinning top
kankibo (iron) wis	a strong vine used for domestic purposes
mountain cow	tapir
pejiballe	(pronounced *picky-by-ah*) small starchy palm fruit
pine	pineapple
ranch	a building or house with a thatched roof, from Spanish *rancho*
sea cow	manatee (whale-like mammal that lives in tropical waters)
sea grape	large grapes that grow in coastal areas
sina	collared peccary (wild pig)
Wa'apin man	'What's going on?' A popular greeting (lit: what happen man?)
wari	white-lipped peccary (wild pig)
wis	vine
yam	giant tuber
yuca	cassava/manioc

English	In three years, he will be ten.
Jamaican Creole	Him ave trii yiez lef fe tun ten.
Spanish	Le faltan tres años para cumplir diez.
Limón Creole	Falta trii yiez im get ten.

Notice how Limón Creole borrows **faltar** from Spanish and uses it without the reflexive *le* in a simplified English form. The phrase **get ten** is similar to the Spanish notion of *cumplir diez*, meaning 'complete ten', instead of the English 'will be ten'.

Words in Limón Creole that are derived from English vocabulary don't necessarily have the same meaning. **All right** often means 'hello' and **OK** can mean 'thank you' or 'goodbye'. **Es que** (lit: it's that), which basically means 'ummm', is a common way to begin a sentence, as shown in this excerpt from Trevor Purcell's book *Banana Fallout*:

> Es que, you know Doña, the rain going start soon so you mus get you hijo them to clean an fork the finca fore it start. The lluvia man, pronto. Once it start you no sabe when it goin termina an you can't make plantain stay of the ground too long, them will rotten.
>
> Trevor Purcell, 1993, 'Banana Fallout: Class, Color, and Culture Among West Indians in Costa Rica', *Afro-American Culture and Society*, vol. 12

Notice that the speaker begins with **Es que** and addresses her friend as **Doña** ('ma'am' in Spanish). She also uses **hijo**, 'son', **finca**, 'field/farm', **lluvia** 'rain', **sabe** (from **saber** meaning 'to know'), **termina** (**terminar** means 'to finish'). The language is an interesting hybrid of Jamaican Creole and Spanish. With practice, you can recognize influences in the vocabulary and better understand Limón Creole.

EMERGENCIAS EMERGENCIES

Help!	¡Socorro!
Emergency!	¡Socorro!
Help me!	¡Ayúden me!
Call the police!	¡Llame a la policía/polí!
Where's the police station?	¿Dónde está la comisaría?
It's an emergency!	¡Es una emergencia!
I need assistance!	¡Necesito ayuda!
Could you help me please?	¿Puede ayudarme, por favor?
Could I please use the telephone?	¿Puedo usar el teléfono, por favor?
I want to report an offence.	Deseo presentar una denuncia.
Look out!	¡Ojo/Cuidado!
Fire!	¡Fuego/Incendio!
There's been an accident!	¡Ha habido un accidente!
Call a doctor!	¡Llame a un médico!
Call an ambulance!	¡Llame a una ambulancia!
I'm ill.	Estoy enferma/o.
My friend is ill.	Mi amiga/o está enferma/o.
I have medical insurance.	Tengo seguro médico.
I've been raped.	He sido violada/o.
I want to see a female police officer.	Deseo hablar con una mujer policía.
Could you please organize an official medical examination?	¿Pueden hacerme un examen médico oficial?
Go away!	¡Váyase! (pol)
	¡Véte! (inf)
I'll call the police!	¡Voy a llamar a la policía!
Thief!	¡Ladrón!
	¡Chapulín! (col)
I've been robbed!	¡Me han robado!

EMERGENCIES

My ... was stolen.	Me robaron mi(s) ...
backpack	mochila
bags	maletas
handbag	bolsa
money	dinero
papers	todos mis papeles
passport	pasaporte
travellers cheques	cheques de viajero
wallet	cartera

My possessions are insured.	Tengo seguro contra robo.
I'm lost.	Estoy perdida/o.
I've lost ...	He perdido ...

SIGNS

(COMISARÍA DE) POLICÍA	POLICE (STATION)

DEALING WITH THE POLICE
HABLANDO CON LA POLICÍA

While police are relatively hard to come by in Costa Rica, the flipside is that at least you don't have to worry about being harrassed by them.

I'm sorry (I apologize).	Lo siento; Discúlpeme.
I didn't realize I was doing anything wrong.	No sabía que no estaba permitido.
I'm innocent.	Soy inocente.
I didn't do it.	No lo he hecho yo.
I'm a foreigner.	Soy extranjera/o.
I'm a tourist.	Soy turista.
What am I accused of?	¿De qué se me acusa?
This drug is for personal use.	Esta droga es para consumo personal.

Do I have the right to make a call?	¿Tengo derecho a hacer alguna llamada?
Can I call someone?	¿Puedo llamar a alguien?
I want to contact my embassy/consulate.	Deseo comunicarme con mi embajada/consulado.
Can I call a lawyer?	¿Puedo llamar a un abogado?
I'd like to see a duty solicitor.	Quiero ver a un abogado de oficio.

EMERGENCIES

THE POLICE MAY SAY

¡Muéstreme su ...! cedula licencia de conducir	Show me your ... driving licence
DNI/documentos pasaporte	identity papers passport
¡Identifíquese!	Show me your identification!
¡Muéstreme su permiso/visa de trabajo!	Show me your work permit!
Está usted detenida/o.	You've been arrested.
¡Queda arrestada/o!	You've been arrested.
Vamos a darte una multa.	We're giving you (inf) a fine.
Acompáñenos a la comisaría.	You must come with us to the police station.
Puede no hacer ninguna declaración hasta que esté en presencia de su abogada/o.	You don't have to say anything until you're in the presence of a lawyer.
¿Cuáles son sus datos personales?	What's your name and address?
Le hemos asignado un(a) abogada/o de oficio.	We've assigned you a duty solicitor.

EMERGENCIES

I'll only make a statement in the presence of my lawyer.	Sólo declararé en presencia de mi abogada/o.
I (don't) understand.	(No) entiendo.
Is there someone here who speaks English?	¿Hay alguien aquí que hable inglés?
I'm sorry, I don't speak Spanish.	Lo siento, pero no hablo español.

arrested	detenida/o
cell	celda
police car	furgón policial
judge	la/el juez
lawyer	abogada/o
police court	juzgado de guardia
police officer	policía/polí/paca (col)
prison	cárcel/tao/chorpa (col)

ENGLISH – SPANISH

In this dictionary we have included the definite (la or el, corresponding to 'the' in English) or indefinite article (una or un, corresponding to 'a' or 'one' in English) with each noun. We've chosen either the definite or indefinite article according to the way the word is most likely to be used.

However, note that generally the articles are interchangeable. Thus un abanico, 'a fan', may also be el abanico, 'the fan'. La abuela, 'the grandmother', may also be una abuela, 'a grand mother'. Just remember, el becomes un, while la becomes una.

In this book, feminine (-a) and masculine (-o) endings are separated by a slash. The feminine form appears first:

musician	música/o

When a definite article precedes a noun which can be either feminine or masculine, both forms of the article are given:

the photographer	la/el fotógrafa/o

When the feminine form of a word is formed by adding -a to the masculine form, -a is given in parentheses.

a curator	un(a) conservador(a)

A

able (to be); can (able)	poder; ser capaz de

Can I take your photo?
¿Puedo sacar una foto?

Can you show me on the map?
¿Me puede mostrar en el mapa?

aboard	a bordo
abortion	el aborto
above	arriba; sobre; encima de
abroad	en el extranjero/ exterior
to accept	aceptar
accident	un accidente
accommodation	el alojamiento
acid (drug)	LSD/ácidos
across	a través de
activist	un(a) activista
actor	un(a) actriz/actor
addict	un adicto
addiction	la drogadicción/ dependencia
address	la dirección
to admire	admirar
admission	la entrada
to admit	admitir
adult	un(a) adulta/o
advantage	una ventaja
advice	el consejo
aerogram	un aerograma

aeroplane	el avión
to be afraid of	tener miedo de
after	después de
(in the) afternoon	(por la) tarde
this afternoon	esta tarde
again	otra vez
against	contra
age	la edad
aggressive	agresiva/o
(a while) ago	hace (un rato)
to agree	estar de acuerdo

I don't agree.
No estoy de acuerdo.

agriculture	la agricultura
ahead	delante/adelante
aid (help)	la ayuda
AIDS	el SIDA
air	el aire
air-conditioned	con aire acondicionado
air mail	por vía aérea
airport	el aeropuerto
airport tax	el impuesto del aeropuerto
alarm clock	un despertador
all	todo
allergy	una alergia
to allow	permitir
almost	casi
alone	sola/o
already	ya
also	también
altitude	la altura
always	siempre
amateur	un(a) amateur; aficionada/o
ambassador	la/el embajador(a)
among	entre
anarchist	un(a) anarquista
ancient	antigua/o
and	y

angry	enojada/o
animals	los animales
annoyed	tener chicha (col)
annual	anual
answer	una respuesta
answering machine	el contestador automático
ant	la hormiga
antenna	la antena
antibiotics	los antibióticos
antiques	las antigüedades
antiseptic	antiséptico
any	alguna/o
appendix	el apéndice
application	solicitud
appointment	una cita
arcades	los portales
archaeological	arqueológica/o
architect	la/el arquitecta/o
architecture	la arquitectura
to argue	discutir
arm	el brazo
to arrive	llegar
arrivals	llegadas
art	el arte
art gallery	el museo de arte
artist	un(a) artista
artwork	una obra de arte
ASA (film speed)	la ASA; sensibilidad
ashtray	el cenicero
to ask (for something)	pedir
to ask (a question)	preguntar
aspirin	la aspirina
asthmatic	asmática/o
atmosphere	la atmósfera
aunt	la tía
automatic teller machine (ATM)	el cajero automático
autumn	el otoño

avenue	la avenida	battery	la batería/pila
awful	horrible	to be	ser/estar (see page 22)
		Be careful!	¡Ojas! (col)
B			
baby	un bebé	beach	la playa
baby food	la comida de bebé	beak	el pico
baby powder	el talco	beautiful	bonita/o; hermosa/o; corrongo (col)
babysitter	el servicio de niñeras		
back (body)	la espalda	because	porque
at the back	detrás de	bed	la cama
backpack	la mochila	bedroom	una habitación
bad	mala/o	beer	la cerveza/birra; una fría (col)
bag	el bolso		
baggage	el equipaje	bees	las abejas
baggage claim	la recogida de equipajes	before	antes
		beggar	un(a) mendiga/o
bakery	la panadería	begin	comenzar
balcony	un balcón	behind	detrás de
ball	la pelota; el balón	below	abajo
ballet	el ballet	beside	al lado de
ballroom	la sala de fiestas; salón de baile	best	la/el mejor
		a bet	una apuesta
band (music)	el grupo	between	entre
bandage	el vendaje	bib	el babero
bank	el banco	bicycle	la bicicleta
banknotes	los billetes (de banco)	big	grande
		bike	una bici (col)
baptism	el bautizo	bill	la cuenta
bar (café)	un bar; una soda (col)	binoculars	los binoculares
		biodegradable	biodegradable
bar with music	una discoteca	biography	la biografía
baseball	el béisbol	bird	el pájaro
basket	la canasta/cesta	birth certificate	la acta de nacimiento
basketball	el baloncesto		
bat	el murcielago	birthday	el cumpleaños
bath/shower gel	el gel de baño	birthday cake	queque de cumpleaños
to bathe	guatearse (col)	bite (dog)	una mordedura
bathing suit	el traje de baño	(insect)	una picadura
bathroom	el baño	black	negra/o

black market	chorizos (col)	box	la caja
B&W (film)	blanco y negro	boxing	el boxeo
blanket	la manta	boy	el chico/niño/flaco/
to bleed	sangrar		loco/ma'e (col)
		boyfriend	el novio
Bless you! (when sneezing)		bra	el sostén
¡Salud!		brakes	los frenos
		branch	la rama
blind	ciega/o	of brass	de latón/bronce
blinker	el intermitente	brave	brava/o
blood	la sangre	bread	el pan
blood group	el grupo sanguíneo	to break	romper
blood test	un análisis de	broken	rota/o
	sangre	breakfast	el desayuno
blue	azul	breast	el pecho
to board	embarcarse	breasts	los senos
(ship, etc)		to breathe	respirar
boarding	la tarjeta de	bribe	un soborno
pass	embarque	to bribe	sobornar
boardshorts	la panta (col)	bridge	el puente
boat	el barco	brilliant	cojonuda/o;
body	el cuerpo		brillante
		to bring	traer
Bon appétit!		broken	quebrada/o
¡Buen provecho!		brother	el hermano
		bucket	un cubo/balde
Bon voyage!		bug	un bicho
¡Buen viaje!		to build	construir
		building	el edificio
bone	el hueso	bull	el toro
book	un libro	bullfighting	los toros
to book	reservar	burn	una quemadura
bookshop	la librería	bus (city)	el bús;
boots	las botas		nave/late (col)
border	la frontera; el límite	bus (intercity)	el autobús
bored	aburrida/o	business	la economía;
boring	aburrida/o		los negocios
to borrow	pedir	busker	un(a) artista del
both	las/los dos		calle
to bother	chingar; agarrar	bus station	la estación/terminal
	chorros (col)		de autobús
bottle	la botella	bus stop	la parada de
bottle opener	el abrebotellas/		autobús
	destapador		
(at the) bottom	(en el) fondo		

busy — ocupada/o
but — pero
butterfly — la mariposa
to buy — comprar

I'd like to buy ...
Quisiera comprar ...

Where can I buy a ticket?
¿Dónde puedo comprar un tickete/boleto?

C

cable TV — el cable
café — una soda (col)
cake shop — la pastelería
calendar — el calendario
calf — el ternero
camera — la cámara (fotográfica)
camera shop — la tienda de fotografía
to camp — acampar
campsite — el camping
can (to be able) — poder; ser capaz de

I can't do it.
No puedo hacerlo.

can (aluminium) — la lata
can opener — el abrelatas
to cancel — cancelar
candle — la vela/candela
canvas — el lienzo
cap (baseball) — la gorra
cape — la capa
car (col) — el carro; la lata
to care (about something) — preocuparse por
to care (for someone) — cuidar de

Careful!
¡Cuidado!/¡Ojo!

cards — las cartas
caring — bondadosa/o
to carry — llevar
carton — el cartón
cash (money) — plata
cash register — la caja registradora
cashier — la caja
cassette — el casete
castle — el castillo; la torre
cat — ln/el gata/o
cathedral — la catedral
Catholic — la/el católica/o
caves — las cuevas
CD — el compact
to celebrate
 (an event) — celebrar
 (in general) — festejar
cemetery — el cementerio
centimetre — el centímetro
ceramic — la cerámica
certificate — el certificado
chair — la silla
champagne — el champán
championships — los campeonatos
chance — la oportunidad
to change — cambiar
change (coins) — el cambio
changing rooms — los vestuarios
channel — el canal
charming — encantador(a)
to chat up — ligar
a cheat — un(a) tramposa/o
to check — revisar
check-in (desk) — el chequeo de equipajes
checkpoint — el control

Cheers!
¡Salud!

cheese — el queso
chemist — la farmacia
chess — el ajedrez

chest	el pecho
chewing gum	el chicle
chicken	el pollo
child	un(a) niña/o; un(a) cría (col)
childminding service	la guardería
children	los hijos/niños
chocolate	el chocolate
chocolate eggs	los huevos de chocolate
to choose	escoger
Christian name	el nombre de cristiano
church	una iglesia
cigarette	un cigarro/ blanco (col)
cigarette papers	el papel de fumar; las boletas (col)
cinema	el cine
citizenship	la ciudadanía
city	la ciudad
city centre	el centro de la ciudad
civil rights	derechos civiles
class	la clase
class system	el sistema de clases
clean	limpia/o
clean hotel	un hotel limpio
cleaning	el trabajo de limpieza
client	la/el clienta/e
cliff	el acantilado
to climb	subir
cloakroom	el guardarropas
clock	el reloj
to close	cerrar
closed	cerrada/o
clothing	la ropa
clothing store	la tienda de ropa
cloud	la nube
cloudy	nublado
clown	payasa/o

coast	la costa
coat	el abrigo
cocaine	la cocaína (coca)
cockroach	una cucaracha
coconut milk	agua de pipa
codeine	la codeína
coins	las monedas
coffee	yodo (col)
cold (adj)	fría/o
a cold	un resfriado/catarro
to have a cold	estar resfriada/o
It's cold.	Hace/Hará frío.
cold water	el agua fría
colleague	un(a) colega
college (US)	el colegio la universidad
(residential)	la residencia de estudiantes
colour	el color
colour (film)	la película en color
comb	un peine
to come	venir
comedy	la comedia
comfortable	cómoda/o
comics	los comics
communist	el comunista
companion	un(a) compañera/o; compa (col)
company	la compañía
compass	la brújula
to complain	estrilar (col)
computer games	los juegos de computador
concert	un concierto
concert hall	el teatro
condoms	los preservativos/ condones
conductor	un(a) cobrador(a)
confession	una confesión
to confirm	confirmar

Congratulations!
¡Felicitaciones!

conservative (person)	conservador(a)
to be constipated	estar constipada/o
construction work	la construcción
consulate	el consulado
contact lenses	los lentes de contacto
contraception	el anticonceptivo
contraceptives	los anticonceptivos
contract	el contrato
convent	el convento

Cool!
Buena nota!(col)

to cook	cocinar
corner (interior)	el rincón
(exterior)	la esquina
corrupt	corrupta/o
to cost	costar/valer
cotton	el algodón
country	un país
countryside	el campo
cough	la tos
to count	contar
court (legal)	el tribunal/juzgado
crafts	la artesanía
crafty	habilidosa/o; ingeniosa/o
crazy	loca/o
credit card	una tarjeta de crédito
cross (religious)	la cruz
cross (angry)	enojada/o
cuddle	un abrazo
cup	una copa
cupboard	el armario
customs	la aduana

to cut	cortar
to cycle	andar en bicicleta
cycling	el ciclismo

D

dad	papá
daily	diariamente
to dance	bailar
dancing	bailando
dangerous	peligrosa/o
dark	oscura/o
date (appointment)	una cita
date (time)	la fecha
to date	citarse; salir con
date of birth	la fecha de nacimiento
daughter	la hija
dawn	la madrugada
day	el día
day after tomorrow	pasado mañana
day before yesterday	anteayer
in (six) days	dentro de (seis) días
dead	muerta/o
deaf	sorda/o
to deal	repartir
death	la muerte
to decide	decidir
deck (of cards)	una baraja
deep	profunda/o
degree (academic)	el título
delay	una demora
delirious	delirante
democracy	la democracia
demonstration	una manifestación
dentist	el dentista
to deny	negar
deodorant	el desodorante

to depart (leave)	partir; salir de
department store	un almacen
departure	la salida
descendent	el descendiente
desert	el desierto
design	el diseño
destination	el destino
to destroy	destruir
detail	un detalle
diabetic	diabética/o
dial tone	el tono
diaphragm	el diafragma
diarrhoea	la diarrea/ cagadera (col)
diary	la agenda
dice (die)	los dados
dictionary	el diccionario
different	diferente
difficult	difícil
dining car	el vagón restaurante
dinner	la cena
direct	directa/o
director	la/el director(a)
dirty	sucia/o
disabled	minusválida/o
disadvantage	una desventaja
discount	un descuento
to discover	descubrir
discrimination	la discriminación
disease	la enfermedad
disillusioned	despijiar
to dislike (someone)	caer en la pura picha (col)
dismissal	el despido
disorder	desmadre (col)
distributor	la/el distribuidor(a)
diving equipment	el (equipo de) buceo
dizzy	mareada/o
to do	hacer

doctor	la/el doctor(a); la/el médica/o
documentary	un documental
dog	la/el perra/o
dole	el bienestar social
door	la puerta
dope	la droga
double	doble
double bed	una cama de matrimonio
double room	una habitación doble
dozen	una docena
dramatic	dramática/o
draughts	las damas
to draw	dibujar/pintar
to dream	soñar
dress	el vestido
drink	una copa
to drink	beber/tomar; echarse (col)
to drive	conducir
driving licence	el carnet; permiso de conducir
drug (prescription)	la medicina
drug dealer	el traficante de drogas
drugs	las drogas
to become drunk	emborracharse
to dry (clothes)	secar
dummy/pacifier	un chupete

E

each	cada
ear	la oreja
early	temprano
to earn	ganar
earring	el pendiente/arete
ears	las orejas
Earth	la Tierra
earth	la tierra

F

English	Spanish
earthquake	un terremoto
east	este
Easter	Pascua; Semana Santa
easter cake	el queque de Pascua
easy	fácil
to eat	comer
economy	la economía
ecstasy (drug)	el éxtasis
education	la educación
elections	las elecciones
electricity	la electricidad
elevator	el ascensor
email	el correo electrónico
embarassed	avergonzada/o
embarassment	la vergüenza
embassy	la embajada
emergency exit	la salida de emergencia
employee	la/el empleada/o
employer	la/el jefa/e
empty	vacía/o
end	el fin
to end	acabar/terminar
endangered species	las especies en peligro de extinción
engagement	el compromiso
engine	el motor
engineer	la/el ingeniera/o
engineering	la ingeniería
English	inglés
to enjoy (oneself)	divertirse
enough	bastante/suficiente

Enough!
¡Basta!

English	Spanish
to enter	entrar
entertaining	entretenido
envelope	el sobre
environment	el medio ambiente

English	Spanish
epoch	la época
equal opportunity	la igualdad de oportunidades
equality	la igualdad
equipment	el equipo
erection	la erección
etching	el aguafuerte
european	un(a) europea/o
evening	la noche
every day	todas los días
example	el ejemplo

For example, ...
Por ejemplo, ...

English	Spanish
excellent	excelente
exchange (money)	el cambio
exchange rate	el cambio
excluded	excluida/o

Excuse me.
Perdón.

English	Spanish
to exhibit	exponer
exhibition	la exposición
exit	la salida
expensive	cara/o
exploitation	la explotación
express	expreso
express mail	el correo urgente/ expreso
eye	el ojo

F

English	Spanish
face	la cara
factory	la fábrica
fall (autumn)	el otoño
family	la familia
famous	conocida/o
fan (machine)	el ventilador

Fantastic!
¡Fantastico!

far	lejos	flag	la bandera
farm	la granja	flat (land, etc)	plana/o
farmer	la/el granjera/o	flea	la pulga
fast	rápida/o	flashlight	una linterna
fat	gorda/o	flight	el vuelo
father	el padre/papá;	domestic flight	un vuelo doméstico
	tata (col)	floor	el suelo
fault (in	un desperfecto	floor (storey)	el piso
manufacture)		flour	la harina
fault (someone's)	la culpa	flower	la flor
faulty	defectuosa/o	fly	una mosca
fear	el miedo	to follow	seguir
to feel	sentir	food	la comida
feelings	los sentimientos	foot	el pie
fence	la cerca	football	el fútbol
festival	el festival	footpath	el camino
fever	la fiebre	foreign	extranjera/o
few	pocos	forest	el bosque
fiancé/e	la/el novia/o	forever	(para) siempre
fiction	la ficción	to forget	olvidar
field	el campo		
fight	la lucha/pelea	I forget.	
to fight	luchar/combatir	Me olvido.	
figures	las cifras		
to fill	llenar	to forgive	perdonar
film (negatives)	la película	fortnight	la quincena
film (cinema)	el cine	fortune teller	adivina/o
film (for camera)	un carrete/rollo	foyer	el vestíbulo
film speed	la sensibilidad	free (not bound)	libre
films	el cine	(of charge)	gratis
filtered		to freeze	helar/congelar
(cigarette)	con filtro	friend	un(a) amiga/o;
(water)	filtrada/o		un(a) compa (col)
to find	encontrar	frozen foods	los productos
fine	una multa		congelados
finger	el dedo	fruit picking	la recolección de
fire (controlled)	el fuego		fruta
(uncontrolled)	un incendio	full	llena/o
firewood	la leña	fun	la diversión; pacho/
first-aid kit	el maletín de		vacilón (col)
	primeros auxilios	for fun	en broma
fish (alive)	el pez	to have fun	divertirse
fish (as food)	el pescado	funeral	el funeral
fish shop	la pescadería	future	el futuro

G

game	el juego
game (sport)	la/el partida/o
garage (mechanic's)	el taller
garbage	la basura
gardening	la jardinería
garden	el jardín
gas cartridge	el cartucho
gate	la puerta
general	general
to get out	jalar/largar (col)
gift	el regalo
gig	presentación
girl	la chica/niña; güila (col)
girlfriend	la novia
to give	dar

Could you give me ...?
¿Podría darme ...?

to give (food or other items)	regalar (col)

Give me ...
Regaleme ... (col)

glass	el vidrio
gloves	los guantes
to go	ir/partir; jalar/largar (col)

Let's go.
Vamos/Vámonos;
Larguemonos. (col)

We'd like to go to ...
Queremos ir a ...

Go straight ahead.
Vaya derecho.

to go out with	salir con
goal	el gol
goalkeeper	la/el portera/o

goat	la cabra
God	Dios
of gold	de oro

Good afternoon.
Buenas tardes.

Good evening/night.
Buenas noches.

Good luck!
¡Buena suerte!

Good morning.
Buenos días.

Goodbye.
¡Adiós!

government	el gobierno
gram	un gramo
grass	la hierba
grave	la tumba
great	fantástica/o

Great!
¡Bueno!

green	verde
grey	gris
to guess	adivinar
guide (person)	la/el guía
guidebook	la guía
guided trek	una excursión guiada
guide dog	perro lazarillo
guinea pig	la quila
guitar	la guitarra
gym	el gimnasio

H

hair	el pelo
hairbrush	el cepillo (para el cabello)
half	media/o
to hallucinate	alucinar

ham	el jamón
hammer	el martillo
hammock	la hamaca
hand	la mano
handbag	el bolso
handmade	hecho a mano
handsome	guapo/bello/chivo/ hermoso
hangover	goma (col)
happy	feliz

Happy Easter!
¡Felices pascuas!

harbour	la ensenada
hard	dura/o
harrassment	el acoso
hat	el sombrero; chonete (col)
have	tener/haber (see page 20)

Do you have ...?
¿Tiene usted ...?

I have ...
Tengo ...

he	él
head	la cabeza
head office	oficina central
headache	un dolor de cabeza
health	la salud
to hear	oír
hearing aid	audífono
heart	el corazón
heat	el calor
heater	una estufa
heavy	pesada/o

Hello.
¡Hola!

Hello! (answering a call)
¿Diga?/Hola.

helmet	el casco

to help	ayudar

Help!
¡Ayuda!

Can you help me?
¿Puede ayudarme?

herbs	las hierbas
here	aquí
heroin	la heroína
high	alta/o
to get high (on marijuana)	pijiarse (col)
high school	el instituto/liceo
to hike	ir de excursión
hiking	la caminata
hiking routes	los caminos rurales
hill	la colina
to hire	alquilar
to hitchhike	hacer dedo
holiday	un día festivo/ feriado
holidays	las vacaciones
Holy Week	la Semana Santa
home page	la página
homosexual	la/el homosexual
honey	la miel
honeymoon	la luna de miel
horny	templado (col)
horrible	horrible
horse	el caballo
horse riding	la equitación
hospital	el hospital
hot	caliente
to be hot	tener calor
hot water	el agua caliente
house	la casa; chante/ choza (col)
housework	el trabajo de casa
how	cómo

How do I get to ...?
¿Cómo puedo llegar a ...?

How do you say ...?
¿Cómo se dice ...?

hug	un abrazo
human rights	los derechos humanos
a hundred	cien
to be hungry	tener hambre
hurt oneself	llevarse (col)
husband	el esposo/marido

I

I	yo
ice	el hielo
ice cream	un helado
identification	la identificación
identification card	el cedula de identificación
idiot	un(a) idiota; basofia/yegua/animal (col)
if	si
ignore	darle aire (col)
ill	enferma/o
immigration	la inmigración
important	importante

It's important.
Es importante.

It's not important.
No importa.

in a hurry	prisa
in front of	enfrente/delante de
included	incluido
income tax	impuesto sobre la renta
incomprehensible	incomprensible
indicator	el intermitente
indigestion	la indigestión
industry	la industria
inequality	la desigualdad
infection	una infección
inflammation	una inflamación
influenza	la gripe
inhaler	el inhalador
to inject	inyectarse; chutarse (col)
injection	una inyección
injury	una herida
inside	adentro/dentro
instructor	la/el profesor(a)
insurance	el seguro
intense	intensa/o
interesting	interesante
intermission	el descanso
international	internacional
interview	una entrevista
intoxicated	estar hasta el culo (vulg)
island	la isla
itch	una comezón
itinerary	el itinerario

J

jack (for car)	un gato
jacket	una chaqueta
jail	la cárcel; el bote/tao; la chorpa (col)
January	enero
jar	una jarra
jaw	la mandíbula
jealous	celosa/o
jeans	los jeans
jeep	un yip
jewellery	la joyería
job	el trabajo
job advertisement	el anuncio de trabajo
job description	descripción del trabajo
jockey	un jockey
jogging	jog/correr

joke	una broma
to joke	bromear
journalist	un(a) periodista
journey	el viaje
judge	un(a) juez
judo	el judo
juice	el jugo
to jump	saltar
jumper	el suéter
justice	la justicia

K

key	la llave
keyboard	el teclado
a kick	un chute; una patada
to kill	matar
kilogram	un quilo
kilometre	un kilómetro
kind	amable
kindergarten	el kinder
king	el rey
kiss	un beso
to kiss	besar

Kiss me.
Bésame.

kitchen	la cocina
kitten	la/el gatita/o
knapsack	la mochila
knee	la rodilla
knife	un cuchillo
to know (of something or someone)	conocer
to know (something)	saber

I don't know.
No lo sé.

L

lake	el lago
lamb	el cordero
land	la tierra
language	el idioma; la lengua
large	grande
last	la/el última/o
last night	anoche
last week	la semana pasada
late	tarde

It's late.
Es tarde.

laugh	reírse/reir
launderette	la lavandería
lavender	la lavanda
law	la ley; el derecho
lawyer	un(a) abogada/o
laxatives	los laxantes
laziness	la pereza; la tigra (col)
lazy	perezosa/o
leaded petrol (petrol/gas)	la gasolina con plomo
leader	un(a) jefa/e; el líder
to learn	aprender
leather	el cuero
leave	abrirse (col)
ledge	el saliente
to be left (behind/over)	quedar
left (not right)	izquierda
left luggage	la consigna
left-wing	de izquierda; izquierdista
leg (body)	la pierna
leg (in race)	una etapa
legislation	la legislación
lens	el objetivo; la lente
Lent	la Cuaresma

ENGLISH – SPANISH

Leo	leo
lesbian	una lesbiana
less	menos
letter	una carta
liar	un(a) mentirosa/o; jetón (col)
library	la biblioteca
lice	los piojos
lie	yuca (col)
to lie	mentir
life	la vida
lift (elevator)	el ascensor
light	la luz
light (adj)	liviano; leve; ligera/o
light bulb	la bombilla; el foco
light metre	el fotómetro
lighter	el encendedor
to like	apreciar/gustar(le)
line	la línea
lips	los labios
to listen	escuchar
little (small)	pequeña/o; poca/o
a little	un poquito
to live (life)	vivir
to live (somewhere)	vivir
to live the good life	tirársela rico (col)
Long live ...!	¡Arriba ...!; ¡Viva!
local	local
location	la localidad
lock	la cerradura
to lock	cerrar
long	larga/o
long distance	de larga distancia
coach	autobús
to look	mirar
to look after	cuidar
to look for	buscar
to look like (someone)	(ser) cagadito (col)

lookout point	un mirador
to lose	perder
loser	la/el perdedor(a)
loss	la pérdida
a lot	mucho
loud	ruidosa/o
to love	amar/querer
lover	la/el amante
low	baja/o
loyal	leal
luck	la suerte
lucky	afortunada/o
luggage (lockers)	(la consigna para) el equipaje
lump	un bulto
lunch	el almuerzo; la comida
lunchtime	la hora de comer
luxury	el lujo

M

machine	una máquina
mad	loca/o
made (of)	estar hecho de
magazine	una revista
magician	la/el maga/o
mail	el correo
mailbox	el buzón
main road	la carretera
main square	la Plaza Mayor
majority	la mayoría
to make	hacer/fabricar
make-up	el maquillaje
man	un hombre
manager	la/el jefa/e; gerente
many	muchas/os
map	un mapa

Can you show me on the map?
¿Lo puede mostrar en el mapa?

margarine	la margarina
marijuana	la marihuana; la mota/mecha (col)

marital status — el estado civil
market — el mercado
marriage — el matrimonio
to marry — casarse
marvellous — maravillosa/o
mass — la misa
massage — el masaje
mat — la esterilla
match (game) — el partido
matches — los fósforos

It doesn't matter.
No importa.

What's the matter?
¿Qué pasa?

mattress — el colchón
mayor — la/el alcalde
mechanic — un(a) mecánica/o
medicine — la medicina;
el medicamento
meditation — la meditación
to meet — encontrar
member — el miembro
menstruation — la menstruación
menu — un menú; la carta
a mess — despiche
message — un mensaje
metal — el metal
meteor — el meteorito
metre — el metro
midnight — la medianoche
migraine — una migraña
milk — la leche
millimetre — un milímetro
million — un millón
mind — la mente
mineral water — el agua mineral
a minute — un minuto

In (five) minutes.
Dentro de (cinco) minutos.

mirror — el espejo

miscarriage — un aborto natural
to miss (feel absence) — extrañar
mistake — un error
to mix — mezclar
mobile phone — el teléfono móbil
modem — un módem
moisturiser — la crema hidratante
monastery — el monasterio
money — el dinero; güevo/
harina (col)
money exchange — el cambio
monk — el monje
monkey — el mono
month — el mes
monument — el monumento
moon — la luna
more — más
morning — mañana

Good morning.
¿Cómo amaneció? (col)

mosque — la mezquita
mother — la madre/mamá
motorboat — una motora
motorcycle — una motocicleta/
moto
motorway (tollway) — una autopista
mountain — la montaña
mountain path — el sendero
mouse — el ratón
mouth — la boca
movie — la película;
cinta (col)
mud — el lodo
Mum — Mamá
muscle — el músculo
museum — el museo
music — la música
musician — un(a) música/o

N

naked	desnudo; chinga/o (col)
name	el nombre
nappy	un pañal
national park	el parque nacional
nationality	la nacionalidad
nature	la naturaleza
nausea	la náusea
near	cerca
necessary	necesaria/o
necklace	un collar; una cadena
to need	necesitar; ocupar (col)
needle	
(sewing)	una aguja
(syringe)	la jeringa
neither	tampoco
net	la red
never	nunca
new	nueva/o
news	las noticias
newsagency	el quiosco
newspaper	un periódico
New Year's Day	el año nuevo
New Year's Eve	la Nochevieja
next	próxima/o
next to	al lado de
next week	la semana que viene
next year	el año que viene
nice	simpática/o; agradable
nickname	un apodo
night	la noche
noise	el ruido
noisy	ruidosa/o
non-fiction	el ensayo
none	nada
noon	el mediodía
north	el norte
nose	la nariz

notebook	un cuaderno
nothing	nada
not yet	todavía no
novel	la novela
now	ahora
nun	una monja
nurse	un(a) enfermera/o

O

obvious	obvia/o; evidente
ocean	el océano

Of course!
¡Por supuesto!; ¡Claro!; ¡Ni mates! (col)

offence	una ofensa/ infracción
(traffic)	
office	la oficina
office work	el trabajo de oficina
office worker	un(a) oficinista
often	a menudo
oil (cooking)	el aceite
oil (crude)	el petróleo

OK.
OK; de acuerdo.

old	vieja/o
olive oil	el aceite de oliva
olives	las aceitunas
Olympic Games	los juegos olímpicos
omelette	el omelete; la tortilla
on	en/sobre
on time	a tiempo
once	una vez
one	uno/un(a)
one-way (ticket)	un (tickete/boleto) de ida; sencillo
only	sola/o; solamente
open	abierta/o
to open	abrir
opening	la inauguración

opera (house)	(el teatro de) la ópera	painter	un(a) pintora/pintor
		painting (the art)	la pintura
operation	una operación	paintings	los cuadros
operator	un(a) operadora	a pair	un par
opinion	la opinión	palace	el palacio
opposite	opuesta/o	pan	una cazuela/ cacerola
optician	un(a) óptica/o		
or	o	pap smear	una citología
oral	oral	paper	el papel
orange (fruit)	una naranja	paraplegic	parapléjica/o
orchestra	la orquesta	parcel	un paquete; una encomienda
order	el orden		
to order	ordenar	parents	los padres
ordinary	corriente/normal	park	un parque
organise	organizar	to park (car)	estacionar
orgasm	el orgasmo	parliament	el parlamento
original	el original	parrot	el loro
other	otra/o	part	una parte
otter	la nutria	party	la fiesta
outside	el exterior; fuera	to party	enfiestarse (col)
over	sobre	pass	un pase
overcoat	un abrigo	passenger	un pasajero
overhead projector	proyector (de transparencias)	passive	pasiva/o
		passport	el pasaporte
overdose	una sobredosis	passport number	el número de pasaporte
to owe	deber		
owner	la/el dueña/o	past	el pasado
ox	el buey	path	el sendero
oxygen	el oxígeno	patient (adj)	paciente
ozone layer	la capa de ozono	to pay	pagar

P

Pay attention! ¡Vea! (col)

pacifier/dummy	un chupete/chupón	payment	un pago
package	un paquete	peace	la paz
packet (of cigarettes)	un paquete; una cajetilla	peak	la cumbre/cima
		pedestrian	un(a) peatón
padlock	el candado	pen	el lapicero
page	una página	pencil	un lápiz
a pain	un dolor	penicillin	la penicilina
painkillers	los analgésicos	penis	el pene
to paint	pintar	penknife	la navaja

pensioner	un(a) pensionada/o	place of birth	el lugar de nacimiento
people	la gente		
pepper	la pimienta	plain	la llanura
per cent	por ciento	plane	el avión
performance	la actuación	planet	el planeta
perhaps	quizás; tal vez; al rato (col)	plant	una planta
		to plant	sembrar
period pain	el dolor menstrual	plastic	el plástico
performing artist	artista callejero	plate	un plato
		platform	el andén
permanent	permanente	play	la obra/pieza
permission	el permiso	to play	
permit	el permiso	(sport/games)	jugar
person	una persona; gente (col)	(music)	tocar
		(col)	darle
personality	la personalidad	to play cards	jugar a cartas
to perspire	sudar	plug (bath)	un tapón
petition	una petición	(electrical)	un enchufe
petrol	la gasolina	pocket	el bolsillo
pharmacy	la farmacia	poetry	la poesía
phone book	una guía telefónica	point (tip)	el punto
phone box	la cabina telefónica	to point	apuntar
phonecard	la tarjeta de teléfono	police	la policía/polí; paca/tomba (col)
photo	una fotografía; foto	police officer	el paco/tombo (col)
		politics	la política
		pollution	la contaminación
		pool (swimming)	la piscina
		(game)	el billar/pool
		poor	pobre
		popcorn	las palomitas (de maíz)
photographer	un(a) fotógrafa/o		
photography	la fotografía	popular magazines	las revistas populares
pickaxe	una piqueta		
to pick up	levantar/agarrar	port	el puerto
pie	un pastel	portrait sketcher	caricaturista
piece	el pedazo/trozo	possible	posible
pig	el cerdo		
pill	una pastilla		
the Pill	la píldora		
pillow	la almohada		
pillowcase	una funda (de almohada)		
pine	el pino	postcard	la postal
pipe	una pipa	post code	el código postal
place	el lugar/sitio	postage	el franqueo

Can (May) I take a photo?
¿Puedo sacar una foto?

It's (not) possible.
(No) es posible.

poster	un póster
post office	Correos
pot (ceramic)	la olla
pot (dope)	la mota
pottery	la cerámica
poverty	la pobreza
power	el poder
prayer	una oración
to prefer	preferir
pregnant	embarazada
pre-menstrual tension	la tensión premenstrual
to prepare	preparar
present (gift) (time)	un regalo el presente
presentation	presentación
presenter	un(a) presentador(a)
president	la/el presidenta/e
pretty	bonita/o
prevent	prevenir
price	el precio
pride	el orgullo
priest	un sacerdote
prison	la cárcel/prisión
prisoner	un(a) prisionera/o
private	privada/o
private hospital	la clínica; el hospital privado
privatisation	la privatización
to produce	producir
profession	una profesión
profit	el beneficio
profitability	rentabilidad
program	el programa
projector	el proyector
promise	una promesa
proposal	una propuesta
to protect	proteger
protected forest	el bosque protegido

protected species	las especies protegidos
protest	una protesta
to protest	protestar
public toilet	los baños públicos
to pull	jalar/tirar
pump	la bomba
puncture	un ponchado
to punish	castigar
pure	pura/o
to push	empujar
to put	poner

Q

qualifications	las calificaciones
quality	la calidad
quarrel	una pelea/riña
quarter	un cuarto
question	una pregunta
to question	preguntar
question (topic)	el asunto; la cuestión
queue	una cola/fila
quick	rápida/o
quiet (adj)	tranquila/o; silenciosa/o
quiet	la tranquilidad
to quit	dejar

R

race (genetic) (sport)	la raza la carrera
racism	el racismo
racquet	una raqueta
radiator	el radiador
railroad	el ferrocarril
railway station	la estación
rain	la lluvia
rally	una concentración
rape	la violación
rare	rara/o

a rash	la irritación
rat	una rata
raw	cruda/o
razor	la afeitadora
razor blades	las hojas de afeitar
to read	leer
ready	lista/o

Are you ready?
¿Está lista/o?

to realise	darse cuenta de
reason	la razón; el motivo
receipt	el recibo
to receive	recibir
recent(ly)	reciente(mente)
to recognise	reconocer
to recommend	recomendar
record	un disco
record shop	la tienda de discos
recyclable	reciclable
recycling bin	el contenedor de reciclaje
red	roja/o
referee	el árbitro
references	las referencias
reflection	
(mirror)	el reflejo
(thinking)	la reflexión
refrigerator	una nevera/ heladera; un refri (col)
refugee	un(a) refugiada/o
refund	un reembolso
to refund	reembolsar
to refuse	negar(se)
regional	regional
registered mail	el correo certificado
to regret	lamentar
relationship	la relación
to relax	relajar
religion	la religión

religious procession	la procesión religiosa
to remember	recordar
remote	remota/o
remote control	el control remoto
rent	el alquiler
to rent	alquilar
to repeat	repetir

Could you repeat that please?
¿Puede repetirlo, por favor?

republic	una república
reservation	una reserva
to reserve	reservar
respect	el respeto
rest (relaxation)	el descanso
(what's left)	el resto
to rest	descansar
restaurant	un restaurante
résumé	curriculum/currículo
retired	pensionada/o
to return	volver/regresar
return (ticket)	(un tickete/boleto) de ida y vuelta
review	la crítica
rhythm	el ritmo
rich (wealthy)	rica/o; andar papuda/o (col)
right (correct)	correcta/o; exacta/o
(not left)	derecha
to be right	tener razón

You're right.
Tienes razón.

right now	en este momento
right-wing	derechista
ring (on finger)	el anillo
(of phone)	la llamada

I'll give you a ring.
Te llamaré.

ring (sound)	el sonido

rip-off	una estafa
to rip someone off	chulear (col)
risk	un riesgo
river	el río
road (main)	la carretera
road map	el mapa de carreteras
to rob	robar
rock	la roca
rock climbing (wall of) rock	la escalada un peñón
rock group	un grupo de rock
to roll (a joint or cigarette)	enrular (col)
rolling	de liar
romance	el amor
room (hotel) (anywhere)	una habitación un cuarto
room number	el número de la habitación
rope	la cuerda
round	redonda/o
rowing	el remo
rowing machine	la máquina de remar
rubbish	la basura
rug	una alfombra
ruins	las ruinas
rules	las reglas
to run	correr

S

sad	triste; agüevarse (col)
saddle	el sillín
safe (adj)	segura/o
safe	una caja fuerte
safe sex	el sexo seguro
saint	santa/o
saint's day	el santo

salary	el salario
(on) sale	estar en venta
sales department	el departamento de ventas
salt	la sal
same	la/el misma/o
sand	la arena
sanitary napkins	las compresas; toallas femeninas
sandals (flip-flops)	las sandalias; las chanclas/ chancletas (col)
satellite dish	la antena parabólica
sauna	el sauna
to save (money)	salvar/ahorrar
to say	decir
to scale (climb)	trepar/escalar
scarf	el pañuelo/la bufanda
school	la escuela
science	las ciencias
scientist	un(a) científica/o
scissors	las tijeras
to score	marcar
screen	la pantalla
script	el guión
scuba diving	buceó
sculptor	un(a) escultor(a)
sculpture	la escultura
sea	el mar
seasick	mareada/o
seaside	la costa
seat	un asiento
seatbelt	el cinturón de seguridad
second	un segundo
second (2nd)	segunda/o
secondary school	instituto/colegio/ secundario
secretary	un(a) secretaria/o
to see	ver

We'll see!
Ya veremos!

I see. (understand)
Ya entiendo.

See you later.
Hasta luego;
¡La/O veo!/¡Las/Os veo! (col)

selfish	egoísta
self-service	el autoservicio
to sell	vender
to send	enviar
sensible	juiciosa/o
sentence	
(grammatical)	una frase
(judiciary)	una sentencia
to separate	separar
series	una serie
serious	seria/o

Seriously!
¡Al chile!; ¡De por derecho! (col)

Seriously?
¿Al chile?; ¿De por derecho? (col)

service	
(assistance)	el servicio
(religious)	el oficio
several	varias/os
to sew	coser
sex	el sexo
sexism	el sexismo
shade/shadow	la sombra
shampoo	el champú
shape	la forma
to share (with)	compartir
shirt	chamís (col)
shit	caca
to shit	cagar
to shave	afeitarse
shaving foam	la espuma de afeitar
she	ella
sheep	una oveja

sheet (bed)	la sábana
.sheet (of paper)	una hoja
shell	una concha
shelves	las estanterías
ship	un barco
to ship	enviar/transportar
shirt	una camisa
shoe shop	la zapatería
shoes	los zapatos; cachos (col)
to shoot	disparar
shop	una tienda
to go shopping	ir de compras
short (length)	corta/o
short (height)	baja/o
short films	los cortos
short stories	los cuentos
shortage	una escasez
shorts	los pantalones cortos
to shout	gritar
a show	un espectáculo
to show	mostrar

Can you show me on the map?
¿Me lo puede mostrar en el mapa?

shower	la ducha
shrine	la capilla
(in a church)	el altar
to shut	cerrar
shuttle	la transbordador espacial
shy	tímida/o
sick	enferma/o
a sickness	una enfermedad
side	el lado
sign	la señal
to sign	firmar
signature	la firma
silk	la seda
of silver	de plata
similar	similar
simple	sencilla/o

sin	un pecado	solid	sólida/o
since (May)	desde (mayo)	some	algún; algunas/os
to sing	cantar	somebody	alguien
singer	un(a) cantante	something	algo
single (person)	soltera/o	sometimes	a veces;
single (unique)	sola/o; única/o		de vez en cuando
single room	una habitación	son	el hijo
	individual	song	la canción
sister	una hermana	soon	pronto
to sit	sentarse	sore throat	un dolor de
size (of	el tamaño		garganta
anything)			
size (clothes)	la talla	I'm sorry.	
size (shoes)	el número	Lo siento.	
skiing	el esquí		
to ski	esquiar	sound	el sonido
skin	la piel	south	sur
skip class	echarsela (col)	souvenir	un recuerdo
skirt	una falda	souvenir shop	la tienda de
skis	los esquíes		recuerdos
sky	el cielo	space	el espacio
to sleep	dormir; ruliar (col)	Spanish	español(a)
sleeping bag	un saco de dormir	to speak	hablar
sleeping pills	las pastillas para	special	especial
	dormir	specialist	un(a) especialista
sleepy	tener sueño	speed	la velocidad
slide (film)	la diapositiva	speed limit	el límite de
slow(ly)	despacio		velocidad
small	pequeña/o	spicy	picante
smell	un olor	spider	una araña
to smell	oler	sport	los deportes
to smile	sonreír	sprain	una torcedura
to smoke	fumar	spring (season)	la primavera
snake	la serpiente/	(coil)	el muelle
	culebra	square (shape)	un cuadr(ad)o
snow	la nieve	(town)	la plaza
soap	el jabón	stadium	el estadio
soap opera	una telenovela	stage	el escenario
soccer	el fútbol	stairway	la escalera
social sciences	las ciencias sociales	stamps	los sellos
social welfare	el bienestar social	to stand	dejar (a alguien)
socialist	un(a) socialista	someone up	plantada/o (col)
socks	los calcetines	standard (usual)	normal

S

standard of living	el nivel de vida
stars	las estrellas
to start	comenzar
station	la estación
statue	la estatua
to stay (remain)	quedarse
to stay (somewhere)	quedarse/ hospedarse
STD	una enfermedad de transmisión sexual
to steal	robar
steam	el vapor
steep	escarpada/o
step	un paso
stockings	las medias
stomach	el estómago
stomachache	un dolor de estómago
stone	una piedra
stoned	ciega/o
stop	una parada
to stop	parar
Stop! ¡Parada!	
storm	una tormenta
story	un cuento
stove	la estufa/cocina
straight	recta/o; derecha/o
strange	extraña/o
stranger	un(a) extranjera/o
street	la calle; el paseo
street demonstration	una manifestación/ demonstration
strength	la fuerza
strike (long-term)	la huelga
(short-term)	el paro
string	la cuerda
stroll	el paseo
strong	fuerte

stubborn	testaruda/o
student	un(a) estudiante
studio	un estudio
stupid	estúpida/o
style	el estilo
subtitles	los subtítulos
suburb	el barrio
success	el éxito
to suffer	sufrir
sugar	el azúcar
suitcase	la maleta/valija
summer	el verano
sun	el sol
sunblock	la crema solar; el bronceador
sunburn	una quemadura de sol
sunglasses	las gafas de sol
sunny	hace sol
sunrise	el amanecer
sunset	la puesta del sol; el atardecer
sunstroke	una insolación
supermarket	el supermercado
Sure. Claro.	
to surf	sorfear/surfear
surface mail	por vía terrestre
surfboard	la tabla de surf
surfer	surfo/surfeador
surname	el apellido
a surprise	una sorpresa
to survive	sobrevivir
sweet	dulce
to swim	nadar
swimming	la natación
swimming pool	la piscina
swimsuit	el traje de baño
sympathetic	comprensiva/o
syringe	la jeringa/(chuta)

D
I
C
T
I
O
N
A
R
Y

T

table	la mesa
table tennis	el ping pong
tail	el rabo; la cola
to take (away)	llevar
to take (food; the train)	tomar
to take photographs	hacer/tomar fotos
to talk	hablar
tall	alta/o
tampons	los tampones
tasty	sabrosa/o
tax	los impuestos
taxi stand	la parada de taxis
teacher	un(a) profesor(a)
teaching	la enseñanza
team	el equipo
tear (crying)	una lágrima
technique	la técnica
teeth	los dientes
telegram	un telegrama
telephone	el teléfono
to telephone	llamar (por teléfono)
telephone office	la central telefonica
television	la televisión
temperature (fever)	la fiebre
(weather)	la temperatura
temple	un templo
ten	diez
tennis	el tenis
tent	una carpa
terrible	terrible
test	una prueba
testicles	güevos (col)
to thank	dar gracias

Thank you.
Gracias.

theatre	el teatro

they	ellas/ellos
thick	gruesa/o
thief	un ladrón
thin	delgada/o
thing (general)	un chunche (col)
to think	pensar
third	un tercio
thirst	la sed

I'm thirsty.
Tengo sed.

thought	un pensamiento
throat	la garganta
ticket	un tickete/boleto
ticket (theatre)	la entrada
ticket collector	la/el revisor(a)
ticket machine	la venta automática de ticketes
ticket office	la boleteria
tide	la marea
tight	apretada/o
time	el tiempo

What time is it?
¿Qué hora es?

timetable	el horario
tin (can)	la lata
tin opener	el abrelatas
tip (gratuity)	una propina
tired	cansada/o
tissues	los kleenex
toast	la tostada
tobacco (kiosk)	el (quiosco de) tabaco
today	hoy
together	juntas/os
toilet paper	el papel higiénico
toilets	los servicios
tomorrow	mañana
tonight	esta noche
too (as well)	también
too much	demasiado

tooth (front)	el diente
tooth (back)	la muela
toothache	el dolor de muelas
toothbrush	el cepillo de dientes
toothpaste	la pasta de dientes
torch	una linterna; un foco
tortoise	una tortuga
to touch	tocar
tour	una excursión
tourist	un(a) turista
tourist information office	la oficina de turismo
tournament	el torneo
towards	hacia
towel	una toalla
tower	una torre
town (large, city)	una ciudad
town (small)	un pueblo
track (footprints) (path)	las huellas el sendero
traffic	el tráfico
traffic lights	los semáforos; las paradas
trail (route)	el camino/sendero
train	el tren
train station	la estación de tren
tram	el tranvía
transit lounge	el tránsito
to translate	traducir
to travel	viajar
travel agency	la agencia de viajes
travel sickness	el mareo
travel guide	el libro de viajes
traveler	un(a) viajera/o
travelers cheques	los cheques de viajero
tree	un árbol
trek	una excursión
trendy (person)	moderna/o
to trick	darle vuelta a (col)

trip	un viaje
trousers	los pantalones
truck	un camión

It's true.
Es verdad.
That's not true!
¡Varas! (col)

trust	la confianza
to trust	confiar
truth	la verdad
to try	intentar/probar
to try (to do something)	intentar (hacer algo)
T-shirt	una camiseta/ playera; chamís (col)
tune	una melodía

Turn (left/right).
Doble (a la izquierda/derecha).

TV	la tele
TV set	el televisor
twice	dos veces
twin beds	dos camas
twins	los gemelos
two	dos
to type	escribir a máquina
typical	típica/o
tyres	los neumáticos; las llantas

U

umbrella	el paraguas
underpants (men's) (women's)	los calzoncillos las bragas/ interiores
to understand	entender/ comprender
undress	deschingarse (col)
unemployed	desempleada/o

unemployment	el desempleo
universe	el universo
university	la universidad
unleaded	sin plomo
unlucky	andar miada/o (col)
unsafe	insegura/o
until	hasta
unusual	extraña/o
up	arriba
uphill	cuesta arriba
urgent	urgente
to urinate	mear; miar (col)
useful	útil
usher	un(a) acomodador(a)

V

vacant	vacante/libre
vacation	las vacaciones
vaccination	una vacunación
valley	el valle
valuable	preciosa/o
value (price)	el precio
van	una vagoneta/ furgoneta
vegetable	una legumbre
vegetarian	un(a) vegetariana/o
vegetation	la vegetación
vein	la vena
venue	un local
very	muy; bien/más (col)
view	una vista
village	un pueblo/ pueblecito
vine	la vid
vineyard	un viñedo
visa	un visado; una visa
to visit	visitar
vitamins	las vitaminas

voice	la voz
volume	el volumen
to vomit	vomitar
to vote	votar

W

Wait!
¡Espera!

Wait a second!
¡Agüevarse/Suave un toque! (col)

waiter	la/el mesero
waiting room	la sala de espera

Wake up!
¡Poner las pilas! (col)

to walk	caminar
wall (building)	la pared
(dividing)	la muralla
want	querer/desear
war	la guerra
wardrobe	el vestuario
warm	caliente
to warn	advertir
to wash	
(something)	lavar
(oneself)	lavarse
washing machine	una lavadora
watch	el reloj
to watch	mirar

Watch yourself! (threat)
¡Pele el ojo! (col)

water	el agua
mineral water	el agua mineral
water bottle	la cantimplora
wave (sea)	la ola
way	el camino

Please tell me the way to ...
¿Por favor, cómo se puede ir a ...

W

Which way?	
¿Por dónde?; ¿En qué dirección?	
Way Out.	
Salida.	
we	nosotras/nosotros
weak	débil
wealthy	rica/o
to wear	llevar
weather	el tiempo
wedding	la boda
wedding anniversary	el aniversario de bodas
wedding cake	el queque de novios
wedding present	el regalo de bodas
week	la semana
this week	esta semana
weekend	el fin de semana
to weigh	pesar
weight	el peso
weights	las pesas
weirdo	un camote (col)
welcome	bienvenida
well	bien
west	oeste
wet	mojada/o
what	qué
What's he saying?	
¿Qué está diciendo?	
What time is it?	
¿Qué hora es?	
wheel	la rueda
wheelchair	silla de ruedas
when	cuándo
When does it leave?	
¿Cuándo sale?	
where	dónde
Where's the bank?	
¿Dónde está el banco?	

who	quién
whole	todo
why	por qué
wide	ancha/o
wife	la esposa/mujer
to win	ganar
wind	el viento
window	la ventana
window (car; ticket office)	la ventanilla
windscreen	el parabrisas
wine	el vino
winery	la bodega
wing	el ala
winner	la/el ganador(a)
winter	el invierno
wire	el alambre
wise	sabia/o
to wish	esperar
with	con
within	dentro de
without	sin
woman	una mujer; chavala (col)
wonderful	maravillosa/o
wood	la madera
word	una palabra
work	el trabajo; brete (col)
to work	trabajar
workout	el entrenamiento
work permit	permiso de trabajo
world	el mundo
worms	las lombrices
worried	preocupada/o
worth	el valor
wound	una herida
to write	escribir

**D
I
C
T
I
O
N
A
R
Y**

writer   un(a) escritor(a)
wrong   falsa/o

I'm wrong. (not right)
No tengo razón.

Y

year   el año
this year   este año

Yes, it is ...
Sies ... (sí es) (col)

yesterday   ayer
yet   todavía

you (pol)   usted
(inf)   tú
(pl)   ustedes
young   joven
youth (collective) la juventud
youth hostel   un albergue
           juvenil

Z

zebra   la cebra
zero   el cero
zodiac   el zodíaco

In this dictionary we have included the definite article (la or el, corresponding to 'the' in English) or indefinite article (una or un, corresponding to 'a' or 'one' in English) with each noun. We've chosen either the definite or indefinite article according to the way the word is most likely to be used. However, note that generally the articles are interchangeable. Thus un abanico, 'a fan'; may also be el abanico, 'the fan'. La abuela, 'the grandmother', may also be una abuela, 'a grandmother'. Just remember, el becomes un, while la becomes una.

Note that the letter ll is listed within the l listing. This is because contemporary Spanish no longer has the ll listed as a separate letter. If you're using an older dictionary as well, you'll probably find it still listed separately.

The letters ch are considered one letter in Spanish, and therefore come between the letter 'C' and 'D'. When looking for anything with ch in it, remember that it will be listed after the alphabetical listings containing c. For example, enchufe, 'plug' will be after encontrar, 'to meet', not between encendedor, 'electricity' and encima de, 'above'.

The letter ñ is always listed after the letter n. Thus you'll find año, 'year' after all words beginning with an.

In this dictionary, feminine (-a) and masculine (-o) endings are separated by a slash. The feminine form appears first:

| música/o | musician |
| abierta/o | open |

When a definite article precedes a noun which can be either feminine or masculine, both forms of the article are given:

| la/el fotógrafa/o | the photographer |

When the feminine form of a word is formed by adding -a to the masculine form, -a is given in parentheses.

| a curator | un(a) conservador(a) |

A

| a culo pelado | stark naked (col) |
| abajo | below |

un abanico	fan
las abejas	bees
abierta/o	open
un(a) abogada/o	lawyer

D I C T I O N A R Y

a bordo	aboard
el aborto	abortion
un aborto natural	miscarriage
un abrazo	cuddle/hug
el abrebotellas	bottle opener
el abrelatas	can opener
el abrigo	coat
abrir	to open
abrirse	to take off; to leave (col)
la abuela	grandmother
el abuelo	grandfather
aburrida/o	boring
acabar	to end
acampar	to camp
un accidente	accident
el aceite	oil
el aceite de girasol	sunflower oil
el aceite de olivas	olive oil
las aceitunas	olives
acois	here (col)
un(a) acomodador(a)	usher
el acoso	harrassment
un(a) activista	activist
la adicción	addiction
una actuación	performance
adentro	inside

¡Adiós!
Goodbye; Hello! (col)

un(a) adivina/o	fortune teller
adivinar	to guess
la adoración	worship
la aduana	customs
un(a) adulta/o	adult
un aerograma	aerogram
la afeitadora	razor
afeitarse	to shave
los aficionados	fans

un(a) aficionada/o	amateur/ enthusiast
afortunada/o	lucky
las afueras de ...	suburbs of ...
agarrado/a	stingy
agarrar chorros	to mess with (a person) (col)
agarrar hembra	to pick up women (col)
la agencia de viajes	travel agency
la agenda	diary
agradable	nice
agresiva/o	aggressive
un(a) agricultor(a)	farmer
la agricultura	agriculture
el agua	water
el agua caliente	hot water
el agua de pipa	coconut milk
el agua fría	cold water
un aguafuerte	etching
el agua mineral	mineral water
aguantarse un toque	to wait a moment
agüevarse	to be sad; bored (col)
el águila	eagle
una aguja	needle (sewing)

¡Ah bárbara/o!
expresses that you're physically attracted to a person (col)

ahogar	to drown
ahora	now
ahorita	pretty soon (col)
el aire	air
el ajedrez	chess
al chile	adventurous/ daring/ hard-core (col)

¿Al chile?
Seriously?

A

al dele	by foot (col)
al lado de	next to
la/el alcalde	mayor
una alergia	an allergy
la alergia al polen	hayfever
una alfombra	rug
algo	something
el algodón	cotton
alguien	somebody
algunas/os	some
el almacén	general store
la almohada	pillow
el almuerzo	lunch
alojarse	to stay (some-where)
el alpinismo	mountaineering
alquilar	to rent/hire
el alquiler	the rent
al rato	maybe
alta/o	high
la altura	altitude
alucinar	to hallucinate
amable	kind
el amanecer	sunrise
la/el amante	lover
amar	to love
amarilla/o	yellow
a menudo	often
América del Sur	South America
amiga/o	friend
una ampolla	blister
los analgésicos	painkillers
un análisis de sangre	blood test
anaranjado	orange (color)
un(a) anarquista	anarchist
andar en bicicleta	to cycle
andar miado	to have bad luck (col)
andar papuda/o	to be rich (col)
el anillo	ring (on finger)

animal	idiot/jerk (col)
una animalada	stupid/silly (col)
un animal salvaje	wild animal
anoche	last night
anteayer	day before yesterday
antes	before
los anti-conceptivos	contraceptives
antigua/o	ancient
los antigüedades	antiques
las antologías	anthologies
un anuncio de trabajo	job advertisement
el año	year
el año nuevo	New Year's Day
el año pasado	last year
el año que viene	next year
el apellido	surname
el apéndice	appendix
un apodo	nickname
apreciar	to like
aprender	to learn
apretar a	to make out with (someone)
un arrastrado	a stud/ slacker (col)
una apuesta	a bet
aquí	here
una araña	spider
el árbitro	referee
la ardilla	squirrel
la arena	sand
el armario	cupboard
el arnés	harness
arriba	above (col)
¡Arriba ...!	Long live ...!
el arte pre-colombiano	Precolumbian art

la artesanía	handicrafts
un(a) artista representisa	performing artist
el ascensor	lift (elevator)
un asiento	seat
el asunto	question
el atardecer	sunset
a tiempo	on time
el atletismo	athletics
el audífono	hearing aid
un(a) autónoma/o	self-employed
una autopista	tollway
el autoservicio	self-service
la autovía	toll-free motorway
la avenida	avenue
avergonzada/o	embarrassed
el avión	plane
ayer	yesterday
ayer por la mañana/ madrugada	yesterday morning
ayer por la noche/tarde	yesterday evening/ afternoon
la ayuda	aid (help)
ayudar	to help

¡Ayuda!
Help!

el azúcar	sugar
azul	blue

B

el babero	bib
bailar	to dance
el baile	dancing
baja/o	low/short
la bandera	flag
el baño	bathroom

un bañazo	an embarrassing person or thing (col)
una baraja	deck (of cards)
el barco	boat
el barrio	suburb
el barrio viejo	old city
una basofia	an idiot (col)

¡Basta!
Enough!

bastante	enough
la basura	garbage
el bate	bat
la batería	battery/drums
el bautizo	baptism
un bebé	baby
beber	to drink
bendecir	to bless
el beneficio	profit
besar	to kiss

Bésame.
Kiss me.

un beso	kiss
el biberón	feeding bottle
la biblioteca	library
una bici	bike
la bicicleta	bicycle
un bicho	bug; mate/ friend (col)
bien	well; very (col)
el bienestar social	social welfare
el billar	billiards/pool
los billetes (de banco)	banknotes
los binoculares	binoculars
la biografía	biography
una birra	brew/beer
blanca/o	white
un blanco	cigarette (col)
blanco y negro	B&W (film)

C

la boca	mouth
la boda	wedding
un bogui	boogieboard
una boleta	rolling paper
el bolígrafo	ballpoint pen
la bolsa	carrier bag
el bolsillo	pocket
el bolso	handbag
la bomba	gas pump
la bombilla	light bulb; flashlight
bondadosa/o	caring
bonito	beautiful
bordar	to embroider
el bosque (protegido)	(protected) forest
botar el rancho	to throw up (col)
las botas (de montaña)	(hiking) boots
una bota de vino	leather wine bottle
el bote	jail (col)
la botella	bottle
los botones	buttons
el boxeo	boxing
brava/o	brave
el brete	job/work (col)
bretear	to work (col)
brillante	brilliant
una broma	joke
bromear	to joke
la bronquitis	bronchitis
la brújula	compass

¡Qué bruto!
How nasty/rude! (col)

el buceo	scuba diving
un(a) buchón(a)	a glutton (col)
un(a) budista	Buddhist
buena/o	good

¡Buena suerte!
Good luck!

Buenos días.
Good morning.

¡Buen provecho!
Bon apetit!

buena nota	good; cool (col)
el bueye	ox
la bufanda	scarf
el búho	owl
un bulto	lump/speck; backpack (col)
burlarse de	to make fun of
el burro	donkey
buscar	to look for
el buzón	mailbox

C

el caballo	horse; person who plays rough (col)
la cabeza	head
la cabina telefónica	phone box
la/el cabra/o	goat/ram
una cabra	chick/sheila (derogatory)
un cabro	man (col)/mate/ pushover
la caca	shit
un(a) cachorra/o	puppy
un cacho parado	a guy who's horny (col)
los cachos	shoes
cada	each
cada día	every day
caer al chante	to go over to someone's house (col)
caer en la pura picha	to strongly dislike someone (col)
cagada de risa	full of laughs (col)

la cagadera	diarrhoea (col)
(ser) cagadito	to look alike (col)
cagar	to shit
cagar (en alguien)	to scold publicly (vulg)
cagarse	to say something imprudent (col)
la caja	box/cashier
una caja fuerte	safe
la caja registradora	cash register
el cajero automático	automatic teller machine (ATM)
una cajetilla	packet
los calcetines	socks
el calendario	calendar
la calidad	quality
caliente	hot
la calle	street
el calor	heat
los calzoncillos	underpants (men's)
los calzones	underpants (women's)
la cama	bed
una cama de matrimonio	double bed
la cámara	room/camera
la/el camarera/o	waiter
cambiar	to change
el cambio	exchange; change (coins)
caminar	to walk
el camino	trail/route
una camioneta	van
una camisa	shirt
una camiseta	T-shirt
un camote	weirdo (col)
campanear	to spy on (col)
los campeonatos	championships
un campesino	farmer; rural person
el camping	campsite

el campo	countryside/field
¿Hay campo?	Is there room? (col)
el canalete	paddle/oar
la canasta	basket
cancelar	to cancel
la canción	song
la cancha	court
el candado	padlock
cansada/o	tired
cantar	to sing; to tell a secret (col)
un(a) cantautor(a)	singer-songwriter
la capa	cape
la capa de ozono	ozone layer
ser capaz de	to be able; to do (can)
la capilla	shrine/altar
el capote	cloak
cara/o	expensive
la cara	face
un carajillo	youngster (col)
una caravana	van
la cárcel	jail
un cardenal	bruise
el carnet de conducir	drivers licence
el carnet de identificación	identification card
la carrera	race (sport)
la carreta	ox cart
la carretera	main road
el carro	car
el carro de Fernando	to go on foot (col)
una carta	letter/menu
la carta astral	astrological chart
las cartas	cards

el cartón	cardboard/carton
el cartucho de gas	gas cartridge
la casa	house
casarse	to marry
una cascada	waterfall
el casco	helmet
casi	almost
castigar	to punish
el castillo	castle
un catarro	cold
catorce	fourteen
una cazuela	pan
celebrar	to celebrate (an event)
celosa/o	jealous
la cena	dinner
el cenicero	ashtray
la Central Téléfonica	telephone office
el centro de la ciudad	city centre
el cepillo de dientes	toothbrush
el cepillo (para el cabello/pelo)	hairbrush
cerca	near
la cerca	fence
el cerdo	pig
el cero	zero
cerrada/o	closed
la cerradura	lock
cerrar	to close/lock
la cesta	basket
un cerdo	pig; person with bad manners
cerrado	closed-minded person
ch	see separate listing after 'C'
ciega/o	blind; stoned (col)
el cielo	sky/heaven
cien	hundred
la ciencia ficción	science fiction
las ciencias	science
las ciencias sociales	social sciences
un(a) científica/o	scientist
el ciervo	deer
una cifra aproximada	ballpark figure
las cifras	figures
los cigarrillos	cigarettes
un cigarro	a cigarette
la cigüeña	stork
cinco	five
cincuenta	fifty
el cine	film (cinema)
el cine de arte	art films
el cine negro	film-noir
una cinta	tape/movie
el cinturón de seguridad	seatbelt
el circo	circus
una cita	appointment
citarse	to date
una citología	pap smear
la ciudad	city
la ciudad antigua	old city
la ciudadanía	citizenship
clara/o	light
Claro.	Sure.
la clínica	private hospital
la cocina	kitchen/stove
cocinar	to cook
el coche	car
el código postal	postcode
la cola	buttocks/tail
una cola	queue/line
colar	to cut in line (col)
¡No te colas!	Don't cut (in line)! (col)

el colchón	mattress
la colina	hill
un colar	necklace
la columna (vertebral)	spine
combatir	to fight
la comedia	comedy
comenzar	to start
comer	to eat
el comerciante	business-person
la cometa	kite
una comezón	itch
la comida	food
la comida de bebé	baby food
cómo	how

¿Cómo puedo llegar a ...?
How do I get to ...?

¿Cómo se dice ...?
How do you say ...?

¿Cómo amaneció?
Good Morning. (lit: how did you wake up?) (col)

¡Como eres tan agil!
Bullshit! (sarcastic)

cómoda/o	comfortable
un cómodo	sofa/couch
un compa	friend/pal (short for compañero)
el compact	CD
un(a) compañera/o	companion
compartir (un dormitorio)	to share (a room)
comprender	to understand
comprensiva/o	sympathetic
el compromiso	engagement (appointment; to marry)
una concentración	rally

un concierto	concert
un concurso	game show
una concha	shell
un condón	condom
conducir	to drive
el conductor	driver
el conejo	rabbit
con filtro	with filter (cigarette)
confirmar	to confirm
congelar	to freeze

Con mucho gusto.
You're welcome.

conocer	to know (someone)
conocida/o	famous
el consejo	advice
la/el conservador(a)	conservative/ curator
estar resfriada/o	to have a cold
la construcción	construction work
construir	to build
la contaminación	pollution
contar	to count
el contenedor de reciclaje	recycling bin
el contestador automático	answering machine
la contrareloj	race against the clock
el contrato	contract
una copa	drink/cup
el corazón	heart
el cordero	lamb
el correo (certificado)	(registered) mail
Correos	post office
el correo electronico	email
el correo urgente	express mail
correr	to run
la corrida	bullfight

corriente	ordinary
corrongo	beautiful
corrupta/o	corrupt
corta/o	short
cortar	to cut
los cortos	short films
coser	to sew
la costa	seaside/coast
costar	to cost

Cuesta bastante.
It costs a lot.

las costillas	ribs
la crema hidratante	moisturising cream
la crema bronceadora/solar	sunblock
una cría	child (col)
la crítica	review
cruda/o	raw
la cruz	cross (religious)
un cuaderno	notebook
la cuadra	stables
un cuadrado	square
cuadro	square
cuadrar	to like (col)
los cuadros	paintings

¿Cuánto?
How much/many?

cuarenta	forty
la Cuaresma	Lent
cuarta/o	fourth
un cuarto	room/quarter
cuatro	four
un cubo	bucket
una cucaracha	cockroach
las cuchillas/ hojas de afeitar	razor blades
un cuchillo	knife
una cuecha	very small amount (salary); spit (col)

la cuenta	bill
un cuento	story
la cuerda	rope
los cuernos	horns
el cuero	leather
el cuerpo	body
cuesta arriba	uphill
las cuevas	caves

¡Cuidado!
Careful!

cuidar	to look after
cuidar de	to care for (someone)
culiar	to fuck (col)
culiarse a	to rip off (col); take advantage
el culantro	cilantro
la culebra	snake
el culo	ass/rear
la culpa	fault/blame/guilt
la cumbre	peak
el cumpleaños	birthday
un cupón	coupon
el curriculum	résumé

CH

un chamís	shirt or T-shirt
el champán	champagne
un chancho del monte	wild peccary; boar
las chancl(et)as	sandals/ flip-flops (col)
un chante	house (col)
un chapulín	street urchin (col) (derogatory name for street kids)
una chaqueta	jacket

¡Chará!, ¡Characita!
What a shame! (col); Too bad!

un(a) chavalo/a — a man/woman; boy/girl (col)
Chepe — San José (col); nickname for anyone named José
chequear — to check
los cheques de viajero — travellers cheques
la chica — girl
el chicle — chewing gum
el chico — boy
la chicha — drink made with corn
chicha — anger; upset (col)
un(a) chichero/a — cheap bar (col); person who frequents such a bar
chingo/a — naked (col)
chingar — to bother (col)
chinga — cigarette butt; large wooden boat (col)
un(a) chirra — old-fashioned or country person (col)
chiva — pretty (col)/ pleasing
un chonete — hat (col)
un choricero — gangster (col); black marketeer
los chorizos — black market (col); illegal business
la chorpa — jail (col)
una choza — house (col)
chulear — to rip someone off (col)
un chunche — thing (usually small) (col)
el chupete — pacifier; love bite (col)
la chuta — syringe (col)

un chute — kick
un chuzo — nice car

¡Qué chuzo!
What a great car!

D

los dados — dice/die
dar — to give
darle — to play (col)
darle aire — to ignore (col)
darle los viente — to be dumped (from a relationship) (col)
darle por la madre — to kick ass (col); to do something really well
darle vuelta — to trick (a boy- or girlfriend)
darse cuenta (de) — to realize
un dato — piece of information

De acuerdo.
OK.

deber — to owe
débil — weak
décima/o — tenth
decidir — to decide
decir — to say

¿Cómo se dice ...?
How do you say ...?

el dedo — finger
defectuosa/o — faulty
de hoy en ocho — a week from now (col)
dejar plantada/o — to stand someone up (col)
de izquierda/o — left-wing
delante de — in front of

SPANISH – ENGLISH

delantero	forward
de larga distancia	long distance

¡Déle aire!
Give me some space! (col)

delirante	delirious
demasiada/o	too much
demasiada/o cara/o	too expensive
una demora	a delay
dentro de (seis) días	in (six) days
dentro de una hora	within an hour
el departamento de ventas	sales department

¿De por derecho?
Are you serious? (col)

¡De por derecho!
Seriously! (col)

los deportes	sport
un(a) deportista	sportsperson
derechista	right-wing
derecha	right (not left)
el derecho	law
el desayuno	breakfast
descansar	to rest
el descanso	intermission
deschingarse	to undress (col)
descompuesta/o	broken
una descripción del trabajo	job description
descubrir	to discover
un descuento	discount
desde (mayo)	since (May)
desear	to want
el desempleo	unemployment
un(a) desgraciada/o	creep (col)
el desierto	desert

la desigualdad	inequality
desmadre	disorder
el desodorante	deodorant
despacio	slow(ly)
un despertador	alarm clock
el despiche	fun; mess (col)
el despido	dismissal
despijiar	to make (col)/ become disillusioned
después (de)	after
el destino	destination/ destiny
destruir	to destroy
una desventaja	disadvantage

¡De veras!
You don't say!

detrás de	behind

¡De un solo pichazo!
All at once! (col)

un devocionario	prayer book
el día	day
el día de los reyes magos	Epiphany
un día feriado	holiday
diariamente	daily

¡Diay!
greeting used by women (col)

dibujar	to draw
los dibujos animados	animation
el diccionario	dictionary
diciembre	December
los dientes	teeth
diez	ten

¿Diga?
Hello! (answering a call)

la dimisión	resignation
el dinero	money

la dirección	address
directo	direct
la/el director(a)	director
un disco	record
una discoteca	discoteque
discutir	to discuss
el diseño	design
disparar	to shoot
un DIU	IUD
la diversión	fun
divertirse	to have fun
dividir (entre)	to share (between); to divide

Doble a la derecha ...:
Turn right ...

Doble a la izquierda ...
Turn left ...

el doble	double
doce	twelve
una docena	dozen
el dolor	pain
un dolor de cabeza	headache
un dolor de culo	a pain in the ass
un dolor de estómago	stomachache
dolor de muela	toothache
dolorosa/o	painful
domingo	Sunday
dormir	to sleep
dónde	where

¿Dónde está ...?
Where's ...?

dos	two
dos veces	twice
las drogas	drugs
la ducha	shower
la/el dueña/o	owner

E

echar	to toss; to throw (someone in jail) (col)
echarse	to have a drink (col)
echarse (a alguien) al pico	to let the cat out the the bag (col)
echárselo	to be a drunk (col)
la edad	age
el edificio	building
un ejemplo	example
él	he
ella	she
ellas/os	they
el que no llora no mama	you only get what you fight for (col)
embarcar	to board (a ship)
embarcarse	to make a serious error (col)
la embajada	embassy
embarazada	pregnant
el embrague	clutch
la/el empleada/o	employee
empujar	to push
en	on/in
en broma	for fun
el encendador	lighter
encajar	to package
el encaje	lace
encantadora/o	charming

Encantado.
I'm charmed.

el encendedor	lighter
las encías	gums
encima de	on top of
encontrar	to meet
un enchufe	plug (electrical)
en el paro	striking
enero	January
enferma/o	sick

E

enfadada/o	angry
la enfermedad	disease
un(a) enfermera/o	nurse
enfiestarse	to party
enfrente de	in front of
enrular	to roll (a joint or cigarette)
el ensayo	non-fiction
la enseñanza	teaching
entender	understand

(Ya) entiendo.
I see. (understand)

la entrada	ticket (theatre)
entrar	to enter
entre	between
la/el entrenador(a)	coach/trainer
el entrenamiento	workout
entretenido	entertaining
una entrevista	interview
enviar	to send
epiléptica/o	epileptic
el equipaje	luggage
el equipo	team/equipment
el equipo de buceo	diving equipment
el equipo de sonido	sound equipment; stereo
la equitación	horse riding
la escalación	rock climbing
la escalera	staircase
escarpada/o	steep
una escasez	shortage
el escenario	stage
escoger	to choose
escribir	to write
un(a) escritor/a	writer
el escrutinio	counting of votes
escuchar	to listen
la escuela	school

la escuela de kinder	kindergarten
un(a) escultor(a)	sculptor
el esgrima	fencing

¡Eso!
interjection to add emphasis or humor

el espacio	space
la espada	sword
la espalda	back
español	Spanish (adj)
espantársela	to threaten someone so they'll stop bothering you (col)
los especies en peligro de extinción	endangered species
las especies protegidas	protected species
un espectáculo	show
el espejo	mirror

¡Espera!
Wait!

espichar	to ruin (an activity or party) (col)
espicharse	to throw your life away (col)
la/el esposa/o	wife/husband
la espuma de afeitar	shaving foam
el esquí acuático	waterskiing
esquiar	to ski
la esquina	corner
estallada	funny (col)
estallarse	to make yourself laugh (col)
la estación	station
estacionar	to park
el estadio	stadium

D
I
C
T
I
O
N
A
R
Y

el estado civil	marital status
una estafa	rip-off
las estanterías	shelves
estar apretado	to be busy (col)
estar corto	to be overly judgmental
estar en todas	to be well informed
estar güey/ güeyeso	to not have money/ a boyfriend/ a girlfriend; to have received nothing (col)
estar hasta el culo	to be very drunk (col)
este	east
este año	this year
este mes	this month
la esterilla	mat
el estilo	style
el estómago	stomach
las estrellas	stars
el estreñimiento	constipation
estriladera	a complainer/ whiner (col)
estrilar	to complain (col)
estropeada/o	broken
la estufa	stove/heater

¡Es vara!
I'm joking! (col)

¡Esa vara!
It's a bad situation! (col)

una etapa	leg (in race); stage
la eutanasia	euthanasia
una excursión	trek; tour group
una excursión guiada	guided trek
el excursionismo	hiking
el éxito	success
la explotación	exploitation
exponer	to exhibit
una exposición	exhibition
expresa/o	express
una expulsión	send-off
el éxtasis	ecstasy (drug)
extranjera/o	foreign
un/a extranjera/o	stranger
extraña/o	unusual
extrañar	to miss (feel absence)

F

la fábrica	factory
fabricar	to make
fácil	easy
una falda	skirt
una falta	fault/foul

¡Fantástico!
Fantastic!

febrero	February
la fecha	date
la fecha de nacimiento	date of birth

¡Felicidades!; ¡Felicitaciones!
Congratulations!

feliz	happy

¡Feliz cumpleaños!
Happy birthday!

el ferrocarril	railway
festejar	to celebrate
la ficción	fiction
la fiebre (glandular)	(glandular) fever
la fiesta	party
filtrada/o	filtered (water)
el fin	the end
el fin de semana	weekend

la firma	signature
flaca/o	thin person (often used by a female to her boyfriend)
la flor	flower
el foco	flashlight/bulb
(en el) fondo	(at the) bottom
la forma	shape
los fósforos	matches
el fotómetro	light meter
los frenos	brakes
frente a	opposite
fresa	stylish (col)
fría/o	cold (adj)
fría	beer
la frontera	border
la frutería	greengrocer
el fuego	fire (controlled)
fuera	outside
fuera de juego	offside
fuerte	strong
la fuerza	strength
fumar	to smoke
una funda de almohada	pillowcase
una furgoneta	van
una fútbol sala	indoor soccer
el futbolín	table soccer

G

Gacho, ¡Qué gacho!
What a shame!; How terrible! (col)

las gafas de sol	sunglasses
la gallina	hen
el gallito	cockerel
Gallo Pinto	fried rice and beans
la/el ganador(a)	winner
ganar	to earn
el ganso	goose

la garganta	throat
la/el gata/o	cat
un gato	jack (for car)
la/el gatita/o	kitten
un gavilán	hawk
el gel de baño	shower gel
los gemelos	twins
la gente	people
gente	a person (col)
el glaciar	glacier
el gobierno	government
gorda/o	fat
un golpe	a hit/strike; a bruise (col)
goma	hangover (col)
gorila	big, strong man
un grabado	recorded/printed
una grabación	recording

¡Gran cosa!
Big deal! (col)

grande	big
los grandes almacenes	department stores
la granja	farm
la/el granjera/o	farmer
greña	long hair (col)
un(a) greñudo	a person with crazy hair (col)
la/el gringa/o	tourist; North American
la gripe	influenza
gris	grey
gritar	to shout
el grupo sanguíneo	blood group
un guabero	very lucky person (col)

¡Guácala!
Disgusting/Nasty! (col)

los guantes	gloves
el guardarropa	cloakroom

la guardería	children's daycare
guatearse	to bathe yourself (col)
el güevo	(a lot of) money (col)
los güevos	testicles
la guía	guidebook/guide (f)
el guía	guide (m)
la güila	a girl (col)
un guindo	a cliff
el guión	script
un(a) guionista	scriptwriter
el gusano	worm
gustar(le)	to like (it)

H

haber	to have (see page 20)
habilidosa/o	crafty
una habitación (doble)	(double) room
una habitación individual/sencilla	single room
hablar	to talk
hace un rato	(a while) ago
hace (media hora)	(half an hour) ago
hace (tres días)	(three days) ago
hacer	to do/make
hacer	to say/ask/answer (col)
hacer dedo	hitchhike (col)
hacer fotos	to take photographs
hacer una vuelta	to deal with an errand
hacerla toda	to have success; a job well done (col)

hacerle una vuelta	to do a favor
la hamaca	hammock
el hambre	hunger
la harina	flour/money (col)

Hasta luego.
See you later.

¡Hasta nunca!
Get lost!

hasta (junio)	until (June)

Hay niebla.
It's foggy.

hecho a mano	handmade

¡Hecho!
Agreed!

un hediondo	a jerk
un helado	ice cream
helar	to freeze
una hembra	young female
un hijueputa (Hijo de puta)	son of a bitch
el herma	brother (col)
el hermanastro	stepbrother
una herida	wound
la hermana	sister
la hermanastra	stepsister
el hermano	brother
hermosa/o	handsome
la heroína	heroin
un(a) heroinómana/o	heroin addict
el hielo	ice
la hija	daughter
el hijo	son
los hijos/niños	children
el hilo dental	dental floss; thong bikini; g-string (col)
una hoja	sheet (of paper); leaf

las hojas de afeitar	razor blades
¡Hola!	Hello.
un hombre	man
los hombros	shoulders
la hora de comer	lunchtime
la hormiga	ant
hospedarse	to stay (somewhere)
hoy	today
en huelga	on strike
el hueso	bone
los huevos	eggs
¡Qué güey!	What a shame!; That sucks! (col)
las humanidades	humanities

I

los idiomas	languages
una iglesia	church
igual	equal
la igualdad	equality
la igualdad de oportunidades	equal opportunity
No (me) importa.	It doesn't matter (to me).
el impuesto (sobre la renta)	(income) tax
el impuesto del aeropuerto	airport tax
la inauguración	opening
un incendio	fire (uncontrolled)
no incluido	not included
infantil	child's
un informativo	news bulletin
la/el ingeniera/o	engineer
ingeniosa/o	crafty
la Inglaterra	England
el injalador	inhaler

una injuria	an insult
la insolación	sunstroke
el instituto	high school
intentar	to try
los interiores	underpants (women's)
el intermitente	indicator/blinker (car)
el invierno	winter
una inyección	injection
inyectarse	to inject yourself
ir de compras	to go shopping
ir de excursión	to hike
ir	to go
ir güeiso/a	to go solo (col); to go out without money (col)
irle güey	to do badly (col)
una irritación	a rash
irse de fiesta	to go out partying (col)
la isla	island
izquierda	left (not right)
de izquierda; izquierdista	left-wing

J

un jabalí	boar
el jabón	soap
la jacha	a face (with a bad expression)
una jalada	a drag (of smoke)
jalar	to pull; to go (col)
la jama	food; lunch/ dinner (col)
el jamón	ham
un jamonero	a bully
el jardín	garden
la jardinería	gardening
una jarra	jar
jarta	to eat (negative connotation) (col)

K

la/el jefa/e	employer
la/el jefa/e de sección	manager
la jeringa	syringe
la/el jetón(a)	a liar
joder	to fuck around (col); to trick/ bother
la joyería	jewellery
jubilada/o	retired
judía/o	Jewish

¿De que juegas?
Don't be so presumptuous!

el juego	game
los juegos olímpicos	Olympic Games
un(a) juez	judge
la jugada	an issue (col)
un(a) jugador(a)	player (sports)
jugar	to play (sport/ games)
jugar cartas	to play cards
el jugo	juice
un jumas	a drinker/partier
el juzgado	court (legal)

¡Jesús!
Bless you! (when sneezing)

K

| un kilo | kilogram |

L

los labios	lips
el lado	side
el lagarto	alligator; greedy person (col)
el lago	lake
lamentar	to regret
la lana	wool
un lápiz	pencil

el lápiz de labios	lipstick
larga/o	long
largar	to go (col)

¡Larguemonos!
Lets get out of here! (col)

de larga distancia	long-distance
la lata	can (tin/ aluminium); (col) bus
el latón	brass
la lavandería	launderette

¡La/o veo!
See you (sg) later! (col)

¡La voló!
That was stupid! (col)

los laxantes	laxatives
leal	loyal
un leash	surfboard leash
la leche	milk
un lechero	a lucky person (col)
leer	to read
lejos	far
la leña	firewood
los lentes de contacto	contact lenses
las letras	humanities
leve	light (not heavy)
libre	free (not bound)
la librería	bookshop
los libros	books
los libros de viajes	travel books
la licencia de conducir	driving licence
la liebre	hare
el lienzo	canvas
ligera/o	light/fast
lila	lilac/purple

el límite de velocidad	speed limit
limpia/o	clean
un lince	lynx
la línea	line
una linterna	flashlight
el lirio	iris
lista/o	ready

¿Está lista/o?
Are you ready?

Estoy lista/o.
I'm ready.

la llamada	phonecall; ring of telephone
la llanura	plain
la llave	key
llegadas	arrivals
llegar	to come/arrive

¿Cómo puedo llegar a ...?
How do I get to ...?

llegar y hacer	to say/ask/answer (col)
llena/o	full
llenar	to fill
llevar	to take (away); to carry
llevarse	to hurt yourself (col)

Llueve.
It's raining.

la lluvia	rain
el lobo	wolf
loca/o	crazy
loco	guy/male (col)
local	local
un local	venue
el lodo	mud
el loro	parrot
los sin hogar	homeless

las luces	lights
la lucha	fight
luchar contra	to fight
el lugar	place
el lugar de nacimiento	place of birth
el lujo	luxury
luminosa/o	light
la luna	moon
la luna de miel	honeymoon
lunes	Monday
la luz	light

Readers looking for a word beginning with ll should look in the previous listing. In contemporary Spanish, the ll is no longer listed as a separate letter.

M

la macha	blonde or (light-complexioned) female (col)
el mach(ill)o	young male; donkey (col)
el machismo	sexism
la madera	wood
la madrastra	stepmother
la madre	mother
la madrugada	dawn
ma'e	mate (col) (pronounced my)
la/el maga/o	magician
maje	dude (col) (slightly derogatory)
mala/o	bad

¡Mala nota!
(the state of being) bad

la maleta	suitcase
el maletín de primeros auxilios	first-aid kit

M

| la mamá | mother |
| mamar | to suck; to do poorly at something (col) |

¡Manda güevo!
How can it be? (col)

un mandato	term of office; order
la mandíbula	jaw
el mando a distancia	remote control
el manivelas	handlebars
la mano	hand
la manta	blanket
la mantequilla	butter
mañana	tomorrow
la mañana	morning
el mapa (de carreteras)	(road) map

¿Me lo puede mostrar en el mapa?
Can you show me on the map?

la máquina (de tabaco)	(cigarette) machine
el mar	sea
maravillosa/o	marvellous
el marcador	scoreboard
marcar	to score
la marea	tide
mareada/o	dizzy/seasick
el mareo	travel sickness
la mariposa	butterfly
por vía marítima	by sea; sea mail
marrón	brown
el martillo	hammer
más	more; very (col)
el masaje	massage
matar	to kill
la matrícula	car registration
el matrimonio	marriage
la mayoría	majority
mear	to urinate

la media parte	halftime
media/o	half
la medianoche	midnight
las medias	stockings/pantyhose
una media teja	50 Colones bill (col)
la medicina	medicine
la/el médica/o	doctor
un medio galope	canter
medio litro	half a litre
el mediodía	noon
la mejenga	informal game of soccer (col)
la/el mejor	best
la/el mendiga/o	beggar
menos	less
un mensaje	message
la mente	mind
mentir	to lie
un(a) mentirosa/o	liar
los (cigarrillos) mentolados	menthol (cigarettes)
el mercado	market
el mes	month
el mes pasado	last month
el mes que viene	next month
la mesa	table
la meseta	plateau/plant

¡Métaselo entre el culo!
Stick it up your ass! (col)

el metro	metre
mezclar	to mix
la mezquita	mosque
el miedo	fear
la miel	honey
el miembro	member
mil	thousand
un militar	person with radical ideas

un millón — one million
minusválida/o — disabled
mirar los escaparates — window-shopping
un mirador — lookout point
mirar — to look
la misa — mass
la/el misma/o — same
la mochila — backpack
la moncha — hunger (col); the munchies
las monedas — coins
las monedas sueltas — loose change
una monja — nun
un monje — monk
el mono — monkey
la montaña — mountain

¡No se monte ma'e!
Stay off my back, mate!

una mordedura — bite (dog)
la mosca — fly
mostrar — to show

¿Me lo puede mostrar en el mapa?
Can you show me on the map?

la mota — marijuana
el motivo del viaje — reason for travel
mozote — a poser (col)
muchas/os — many
muda/o — mute
el muelle — pier/dock
muerta/o — dead
la muerte — death
una multa — a fine
las muñecas — dolls
las murallas — city walls
el músculo — muscle
el museo — museum; art gallery
una musulman/ un musulmán — Muslim

N

nada — none

No es nada.
It's nothing.

nadar — to swim
una naranja — orange (fruit)
la nariz — nose
la natación — swimming
los naturales — fruit drinks
la naturaleza — nature
la navaja — penknife
un nave — ship; bus (col)
la Navidad — Christmas Day
nebulosa — nebulous
necesitar — to need
negar — to deny
negarse — to refuse
negra/o — black
los neumáticos — tyres
una nevera — refrigerator
un(a) nieta/o — grandchild
la nieve — snow

¡Ni mates!
Of course! (col)

la niña — girl
la niñera/o — babysitter
el niño — boy

¡Ni picha!
Absolutely nothing! (col)

el nivel (de vida) — standard (of living)

la noche — evening/night
la Nochebuena — Christmas Eve
la Nochevieja — New Year's Eve

No estar en nada.
to not know what's happening (col)

¡No haga loco!
Don't be stupid! (col)

O

¡No haga mates! — Don't move! (col)

¡No la/lo atraso! — I don't care (what you think or do)! (col)

el nombre (cristiano)	(Christian) name
el norte	north
nosotras/os	we
las noticias	news
las novelas	novels
novena/o	ninth
noventa	ninety
la novia	girlfriend/bride
el novio	boyfriend/groom
la nube	cloud
nueva/o	new
nueve	nine
el número (de la habitación)	(room) number
nunca	never
la nutria	otter

O

o	or
el objetivo	lens
una obra de arte	artwork
obrera/o	factory worker
obvia/o	obvious
octava/o	eighth
octubre	October
ocupar	to need (col)
ochenta	eighty
ocho	eight
oeste	west
la oficina (central)	(head) office
la oficina de teléfonos	telephone office
un(a) oficinista	office worker
el oficio religioso	service (religious)

¡Ohí! — expression of disbelief (col)

oír	to hear
el ojo	eye

¡Ojo! — Careful!

la ola	wave
oler	to smell
la olla	pot/pan
un olor	a smell
olvidar	to forget
once	eleven
la ópera	opera; opera house
una oración	prayer
la orden	order (command)
el orden	order (placement)
ordenar	to order
la oreja	ear
el orgullo	pride
el oro	gold
las orquillas	orchids
el osíco	mouth (of animal) (col)
oscura/o	dark
el oso	bear
otoño	autumn
otra/o	other
una oveja	sheep

P

la paca	the police (col)
el paco	police officer/ official (col)
pacho	(col) fun
un pachuco	Costa Rican who speaks pachuquismo
pachuquismo	Costa Rican slang

SPANISH – ENGLISH

el padrastro	stepfather
el padre	father
los padres	parents
pagar	to pay
una página	page
un pago	payment
un país	country
el País de Gales	Wales
el pájaro	bird
la pala	shovel; table tennis paddle
las palomitas de maiz	popcorn
la palanca de cambios	gear stick
el pan	bread
la panadería	bakery
la panta	boardshorts
la pantalla	screen
los pantalones	trousers
los pantalones cortos	shorts
los pañales (descartables)	(disposable) diapers/nappies
los pañuelos de papel	tissues
el Papa	Pope
papá	dad
la papa	potato
el papel	paper
el papel de fumar	cigarette papers
el papel higiénico	toilet paper
la papelería	stationers
el papi-fútbol	indoor soccer
un par	a pair
los parabrisas	windscreen
una parada	stop
parar	to stop
el paraguas	umbrella
un(a) parapléjica/o	paraplegic
una pareja	pair (a couple)
un pargo	snapper (fish); 1000 Colones bill (col); lazy person (col)
los parientes	relations
parir	to do difficult work (col)
parlar	talking persuasively (col)
el puro	sirke
un parque de atracciones	theme park
la partida	game (sport)
la partida de nacimiento	birth certificate
el partido	match
los partidos políticos	political parties
partir (de)	to leave (from)
pasado	past
pasado mañana	day after tomorrow
un pasajero	passenger
un pase	pass
un paseo	a stroll
un paso	step
la pasta de dientes	toothpaste
un pastel	pie
el pastel de cumpleaños	birthday cake
la pastelería	cake shop
las pastillas (para dormir)	(sleeping) pills
una patada	kick
los patines	rollerblades
el pato	duck
el pavo	turkey; naive person (col)
la/el payasa/o	clown
la paz	peace
un(a) peatón	pedestrian
un pecado	sin

P

D
I
C
T
I
O
N
A
R
Y

el pecho	chest/breast
un pedazo	piece
pedir	to ask for; to borrow
pegarse una ruleada	to sleep well (col)

¡Pele el ojo!
Watch yourself! (col) (threat, depending on tone)

un peine	comb
una pelea	a quarrel
una película	film
el pelo	hair
la pelota	ball
los pendientes	earrings
el pene	penis
el peñón	wall of rock (crag)
pequeña/o	small
la/el perdedor(a)	loser
perder	to lose
perdonar	to forgive
la pereza	laziness
perezosa/o	lazy
un periódico (en inglés)	(English-language) newspaper
un(a) periodista	journalist
el permiso de conducir	driving licence
el permiso de trabajo	work permit
pero	but
la perra	dog/bitch (derogatory)
el perro	dog
el perro lazarillo	guide dog
pesada/o	heavy/mean (col)
las pesas	weights
el pescado	fish (as food)
el pez	fish

un picado	a buzz (col); slight effect of alcohol
picante	spicy
un picapiedras	stone sculptor
una picazón	itch
un(a) picazón de culo	an annoying person (vulg)
un pico	beak/pickaxe
una picha	penis (vulg)
un pichazo	strong blow; a lot; many (col)
pichuda/o	pretty (col)/ excellent
el pie	foot
la piedra	stone
la piel	skin
la pierna	leg
pijiado	high (col) (on marijuana)
pijiarse	to get high on marijuana (col)
la pila	battery
la píldora	the Pill
la pimienta	pepper
un pinche	miser (col)
el pino	pine
la pinocha	vagina (vulg)
pintar	to paint
un(a) pintor(a)	painter
la pintura	painting (art of)
los piojos	lice
una pipa	pipe, coconut
un pipi	surfing poser (col)
una piqueta	pickaxe
las piquetas	tent pegs
la piscina	swimming pool
el piso	floor (storey)
la pista	race track; tennis court
el placaje	tackle
plana/o	flat (land, etc)

SPANISH – ENGLISH

una planta	plant
plastar	to smash
el plástico	plastic
la plata	silver/cash/money
un plato	plate
la playa	beach
la Plaza Mayor	main square
la plaza	square (in town)
la plaza de toros	bullring
pobre	poor
la pobreza	poverty
un poco/poquito	a little bit
pocos	few
el poder	power
poder	to be able to do; can

¿Podría darme ...?
Could you give me ...?

¿Puede Ud. ayudarme?
Can you help me?

¿Puedo sacar una foto?
Can I take a photo?

el pollo	chicken
poner	to put

¡Ponga la pilas!
Wake up! (col)

un poquito	a little (amount)
por	for
por ciento	per cent

Por ejemplo, ...
For example, ...

porque	because
los portales	arcades
por vía terrestre/ marítima	surface/ sea mail
una postal	a postcard
las postales	postcards
el precio	price
una pregunta	a question

preguntar	to ask (a question)
preocupada/o	worried
preocuparse por	to care (about something)

¡No te preocupes!
Forget about it!; Don't worry! (inf)

preparar	to prepare
los preservativos	condoms
lu presión arterial	blood pressure
la presión baja/ alta	low/high blood pressure
prevenir	to prevent
la primavera	spring (season)
el primer	first
la/el primera ministra/o	prime minister
privada/o	private
probar	to try
la procesión religiosa	religious procession
los productos congelados	frozen foods
los productos lácteos	dairy products
profunda/o	deep
una promesa	promise
pronto	soon
una propuesta	proposal
proteger	to protect
próxima/o	next
el proyector	projector
una prueba de embarazo	pregnancy test kit
las pruebas nucleares	nuclear testing
un puebl(ecit)o	village
el puente	bridge
la puerta	gate
el puerto	harbor/port
la puesta del sol	sunset
la pulg	flea
el punto	point (tip)

¡Pura Vida!
Pure Life! (expresses positivity)

Q

una quebrada — stream

¿Qué?
What?

¡¿Qué?!
What? (col) (informal greeting)

¡Qué colorazo!
How embarrassing! (col)

¡Qué dicha!
expression of happiness (col)

¿Qué hace/s?
What are you (pol/inf) doing?

¡Qué jeta!
I can't believe what you're saying! (col)

¡¿Qué me dice?!
How are you going? (col)

¿Qué pasa?
What's the matter?

¡¿Qué tiene?!
What's the big deal?! (col)

quedar	to be left (behind)
quedarse	to stay (remain)
una quemadura	a burn
una quemadura de sol	sunburn
querer	to want/love

Queremos ir a ...
We'd like to go to ...

el queso	cheese
quince	fifteen
la quincena	fortnight
quinta/o	fifth
el quiosco	newsagency
quitar	to take away; borrow something without permission (col)

R

el rabo	tail
una rata	mouse; traitor (col)
una ratada	action of a negative person (col)
el ratón	rat
el ratonero	buzzard
la raza	race (genetic)
la razón	reason
realizar	to carry out
una rebaja	discount
recibir	to receive
el recibo	receipt
reciente	recent
recientemente	recently
la recogida de equipajes	baggage claim
reconocer	to recognise
recordar	to remember
un recuerdo	souvenir
la red	net
redonda/o	round
reembolsar	to refund
un reembolso	refund
el reflejo	reflection (mirror)
la reflexión	reflection (thinking)
un(a) refugiada/o	refugee
un refugio de montaña	mountain hut
regalar	to give gifts; to give (col)

Regaleme ...
Give me ... (col) (used casually to order food or to buy items)

un regalo	present (gift)
la regla	menstruation
las reglas	rules
regresar	to return

Regular.
OK.

la reina	queen
reírse	laugh
la relación	relationship
relajar	to relax
el reloj	watch/clock
el remo	rowing
la rentabilidad	profitability
repartir	to deal
repartir (entre)	to share (with)
un resfriado	a cold
la residencia de estudiantes	colege
los residuos tóxicos	toxic waste
respirar	to breathe
una respuesta	answer
el retablo	altarpiece
la/el retratista	portrait sketcher
la reventa	ticket scalping
revisar	to check
una revista	magazine
las revistas populares	popular magazines
el rey	king
rica/o	rich (wealthy)
un riesgo	risk
el rincón	corner (interior)
el río	river
una riña	a quarrel
el riñón	kidney
el ritmo	rhythm
robar	to rob/steal

el roble	oak
el rocko	father; old man (col)
la rodilla	knee
roja/o	red
un rojo	1000 Colones bill
el romero	rosemary
la ropa	clothing
rosa	pink
rota/o	broken. torn
rubia/o	blonde
la rueda	wheel
el ruido	noise
ruidosa/o	noisy
ruliar	to sleep (col)
ruliarse	to go to bed (col)

S

¡Salado!
Too bad!; Tough luck! (col)

un sapazo	a gossip (col); big mouth
(para) siempre	forever
el sexo seguro	safe sex
sábado	Saturday
la sábana	sheet
un sabanero	Costa Rican cowboy
saber	to know (something)
un saco de dormir	sleeping bag
la sal	salt
la sala (de espera)	(waiting) room
la sala de fiestas	ballroom

Salida.
Way Out.

la salida (de emergencia)	(emergency) exit

S

las salidas	departures
el saliente	ledge
salir con	to go out with
salir de	to depart (leave)
saltar	to jump
la salud	health

¡Salud!
Bless you! (sneezing)

salvar	to save
san	saint
las sandalias	sandals
sangrar	to bleed
la sangre	blood
la/el santa/o	saint
el sapo	toad
secar	to dry
la sed	thirst
la seda	silk
seguir	to follow
segura/o	safe
el seguro	insurance
seis	six
los sellos	stamps
el semáforo	traffic lights
la Semana santa	Holy Week
la semana (pasada)	(last) week
la semana que viene	next week
sembrar	to plant
el semental	stallion
sencilla/o	simple
el sendero	trail; mountain path
los senos	breasts
la sensibilidad	film speed
sensible	sensitive
sentarse	to sit
sentir	to feel
séptima/o	seventh
ser	to be (see also estar page 23)

seria/o	serious
seropositiva/o	HIV positive
la serpiente	snake
los servicios	toilets
sesenta	sixty
setenta	seventy
setiembre/ septiembre	September
el sexo sano	safe sex
sexta/o	sixth
una señal	a sign
el SIDA	AIDS

Si Diós quiere.
God willing. (col)

siempre   always

Lo siento.
I'm sorry.

Sies (sí es) ...
Yeah, it's ...

siete	seven
la silla	chair
la silla de ruedas	wheelchair
el sillín	saddle
simpática/o	nice; friendly
sin filtro	without filter
sin plomo	unleaded
los sindicatos	trade unions
el síndrome de abstinencia (mono)	cold turkey
el sitio	place
sobornar	to bribe
un soborno	a bribe
sobre	above/on
el sobre	envelope
una sobredosis	overdose
un sobretodo	coat
una soda	small café; soda pop
el sol	sun

sola/o	alone
solamente	only
sola/o	single (unique)
sólo	only
soltera/o	single (person)
la sombra	shade
los sondeos	polls
el sonido	sound
sonreír	to smile
sorda/o	deaf
sorfear	to surf
soñar	to dream
un sostén	bra
suave	smooth/soft/mild

¡Suave!
Chill out! (col)

subir	to go up; to get on; to climb
sucia/o	dirty
la sucursal	branch office
Sudamérica	South America
sudar	to perspire
la suegra	mother-in-law
el suegro	father-in-law
el suelo	ground
la suerte	luck
sufragar	to vote
sufrir	to suffer

¡Por supuesto!
Great!; Of course!

sur	south
un surdo	lefty
un surfeador	a surfer
un surfo	a surfer

T

la tabla de surf	surfboard
el tablero de ajedrez	chess board
un tacaño	miser

el talco	baby powder
la talla	size (clothes)
el taller	garage
el tamaño	size (general)
también	also
tampoco	neither
tan grande como	as big as
un tanto	point (games)
el tao	jail (col)
un tapete	rug
un tapis	a drinker (said among friends); a drink (col)
tarde	late
(de la) tarde	(in the) afternoon
una tarjeta de crédito	credit card
la tarjeta de embarque	boarding pass
la tarjeta de teléfono	phonecard
una tarjeta postal	postcard
la tarta/queque de boda	wedding cake
Tata	father (col)
el teclado	keyboard
una teja	100 (col); 100 Colones
la tele	TV
el teleférico	cable car
una telenovela	soap opera
el telescopio	telescope
el televisor	TV set
estar templado	to feel horny (col)
un templo	temple/church
temprano	early
tener chicha	to be annoyed/ upset (col)
tener prisa	to be in a hurry
tener razón	to be right
tenerla toda	to be well off (col) (financially)

tener	to have (see page 22)
¿Tiene usted ...?	Do you have ...?
tercera/o	third (adj)
un tercio	a third
terminar	to end
el ternero	calf
un terremoto	earthquake
el terreno	location
terrible	terrible
por vía terrestre	surface mail
testaruda/o	stubborn
el tiempo	weather/time
una tienda (de campaña)	tent
la tienda de alimentación	general store
una tienda de artesanía	craft shop
la tienda de casetes	music shop
la tienda de fotografía	camera shop
la tienda de recuerdos	souvenir shop
la Tierra	Earth
la tierra	earth
la tigra	laziness (col)
las tijeras	scissors
el tipo de cambio	exchange rate
el tiro	hit/shot
tirársela rico	to live the good life (col)
tita	affectionate name for a woman (col)
el título	degree/title
un tiquete (de ida y vuelta)	(return) ticket
un tiquete sencillo	one-way ticket
una toalla	towel

el tobillo	ankle
todavía no	not yet
todo	all
tomar	to take (food; the train, etc)
la tomba	the police (col)
el tombo	police officer (col)
toparse con	accidentally meet up with somone (col)
tostada/o	high (on marijuana) (col)
el tomillo	thyme
una torcedura	sprain
el torneo	tournament
el toro	bull
el toro bravo	fighting bull
los toros	bullfighting
la torre	tower
una tortuga	tortoise/turtle
un tos	a cough
un(a) trabajador(a)	manual worker
un(a) trabajador(a) autónoma/o	self-employed
el trabajo	job
el trabajo de oficina	office work
traer	to bring
el traficante de drogas	drug dealer
tragarse la yuca	to swallow a lie (col)
un(a) tramposa/o	a cheat
un traje	a suit
un traje de baño	a bathing suit
tranzar (a alguien)	to trust and like (someone) (col)
trece	thirteen
treinta	thirty

el tren	train
las trenzas	braids
trepar	to climb
tres	three
tres cuartos	three-quarters
el tribunal	court (legal)
un trío	three of a kind
triste	sad
un trozo	piece
tú	you (inf)
tuanis	right on; the state of being positive (col)
un tucán	5000 Colones bill (col)
la tumba	grave

U

la/el última/o	last
un ultrasonido	ultrasound
única/o	single (unique)
una/o	one

Upe!
Hello, is anyone home? (col)

usted (Ud)	you (sg/pol)
ustedes (Uds)	you (pl/pol)
las uvas	grapes

V

va	he/she/it goes
la vaca	cow
vacía/o	empty
vacilar	to have fun (col)
vacilar con (alguien)	to have a good time (with someone) (col)
puro vacilón	all in good fun (col)
valer	to cost

¿Cuánto vale ir a ...?
How much is it to go to ...?

el valle	valley

Vámonos.
Let's go.

el vapor	steam
los vaqueros	jeans
una vara	object/matter/ problem (col)

¡Varas!
That's not true! (col)

varias/os	several

¡Vea!
Pay attention!; Listen up! (col)

veinte	twenty
la vela	candle
la vena	vein
la/el vencedor(a)	winner
un vendaje	bandage
vender	to sell
venir	to come
la venta	ticket
automática de tickets	machine
(estar en) venta	(to be on) sale
una ventaja	advantage
la ventana	window
la ventanilla	window (car; ticket office)
el ventilador	fan
ver	to see

¡Ya veremos!
We'll see!

el verano	summer
verde	green
un verde	studious person (col)

¿¡Ves!?
You see, I'm right?! (col)

el vestíbulo	foyer
el vestido	dress
el vestuario	wardrobe
los vestuarios	changing rooms
una vez	once
de vez en cuando	sometimes
viajar	to travel
el viaje	journey
la vida	life
el vidrio	glass
vieja/o	old
viejo	dude/mate (col)
el viento	wind

¡Vieras!
I wish you could have seen it! (col)

un viñedo	vineyard
la violación	rape
una visa	visa
un visado	visa
la vista	view
un vivazo	person who lives off others
un vividor	person who lives off others
vivir	to live (life/ somewhere)
el volumen	volume
volver	to return

¡Voy jalando!
I'm out of here! (col)

la voz	voice
el vuelo (nacional)	(domestic) flight

Y

y	and
ya	already/now

¡¿Ya, la vio?!
Do you understand now? (col)

¡Ya lo dijo!
End of story! (col)

¡Ya voy!
No way! (col)

la yegua	mare/idiot; stupid girl (col)
un yip	jeep
yo	I
el yodo	coffee (col)
un(a) yonki	junkie
una yuca	manioc/cassava; a lie (col)

Z

la zapatería	shoe shop
los zapatos	shoes
el zarpe	finale/encore; last drink of the evening (col)
el zopilote	buzzard/vulture
la zorra	fox; bitch (vulg)
el zorro	fox

F
I
N
D
E
R

259

F
I
N
D
E
R

Phrasebooks

L onely Planet phrasebooks are packed with essential words and phrases to help travellers communicate with the locals. With colour tabs for quick reference, an extensive vocabulary and use of script, these handy pocket-sized language guides cover day-to-day travel situations.

- handy pocket-sized books
- easy to understand Pronunciation chapter
- clear & comprehensive Grammar chapter
- romanisation alongside script for ease of pronunciation
- script throughout so users can point to phrases for every situation
- full of cultural information and tips for the traveller

'...vital for a real DIY spirit and attitude in language learning'

– Backpacker

'the phrasebooks have good cultural backgrounders and offer solid advice for challenging situations in remote locations'

– San Francisco Examiner

Arabic *(Egyptian)* • Arabic *(Moroccan)* • Australian *(Australian English, Aboriginal and Torres Strait languages)* • Baltic States *(Estonian, Latvian, Lithuanian)* • Bengali • Brazilian • British • Burmese • Cantonese • Central Asia • Central Europe *(Czech, French, German, Hungarian, Italian, Slovak)* • Eastern Europe *(Bulgarian, Czech, Hungarian, Polish, Romanian, Slovak)* • Ethiopian *(Amharic)* • Fijian • French • German • Greek • Hill Tribes • Hindi & Urdu • Indonesian • Italian • Japanese • Korean • Lao • Latin American Spanish • Malay • Mandarin • Mediterranean Europe *(Albanian, Croatian, Greek, Italian, Macedonian, Maltese, Serbian, Slovene)* • Mongolian • Nepali • Pidgin • Pilipino *(Tagalog)* • Quechua • Russian • Scandinavian Europe *(Danish, Finnish, Icelandic, Norwegian, Swedish)* • South-East Asia *(Burmese, Indonesian, Khmer, Lao, Malay, Tagalog Pilipino, Thai, Vietnamese)* • South Pacific *(Fijian, Fijian Hindi, Hawaiian, Kanak, Maori, Niuean, Pacific French, Pacific Englishes, Rapanui, Rarotongan Maori, Samoan, Spanish, Tahitian, Tongan)* • Spanish *(Castilian; also includes Catalan, Galician and Basque)* • Sri Lanka • Swahili • Thai • Tibetan • Turkish • Ukrainian • USA *(US English, Vernacular, Native American languages, Hawaiian)* • Vietnamese • Western Europe *(Basque, Catalan, Dutch, French, German, Greek, Irish)*

COMPLETE LIST OF LONELY PLANET BOOKS

AFRICA Africa – the South • Africa on a shoestring • Arabic (Egyptian) phrasebook • Arabic (Moroccan) phrasebook • Cairo • Cape Town • Central Africa • East Africa • Egypt • Egypt travel atlas • Ethiopian (Amharic) phrasebook • The Gambia & Senegal • Kenya • Kenya travel atlas • Malawi, Mozambique & Zambia • Morocco • North Africa • South Africa, Lesotho & Swaziland • South Africa, Lesotho & Swaziland travel atlas • Swahili phrasebook • Trekking in East Africa • Tunisia • West Africa • Zimbabwe, Botswana & Namibia • Zimbabwe, Botswana & Namibia travel atlas
Travel Literature: The Rainbird: A Central African Journey • Songs to an African Sunset: A Zimbabwean Story • Mali Blues: Traveling to an African Beat

AUSTRALIA & THE PACIFIC Australia • Australian phrasebook • Bushwalking in Australia • Bushwalking in Papua New Guinea • Fiji • Fijian phrasebook • Islands of Australia's Great Barrier Reef • Melbourne • Micronesia • New Caledonia • New South Wales & the ACT • New Zealand • Northern Territory • Outback Australia • Papua New Guinea • Pidgin phrasebook • Queensland • Rarotonga & the Cook Islands • Samoa • Solomon Islands • South Australia • South Pacific phrasebook • Sydney • Tahiti & French Polynesia • Tasmania • Tonga • Tramping in New Zealand • Vanuatu • Victoria • Western Australia
Travel Literature: Islands in the Clouds • Sean & David's Long Drive

CENTRAL AMERICA & THE CARIBBEAN Bahamas and Turks & Caicos • Barcelona • Bermuda • Central America on a shoestring • Costa Rica • Cuba • Dominican Republic & Haiti • Eastern Caribbean • Guatemala, Belize & Yucatán: La Ruta Maya • Jamaica • Mexico • Mexico City • Panama
Travel Literature: Green Dreams: Travels in Central America

EUROPE Amsterdam • Andalucía • Austria • Baltic States phrasebook • Berlin • Britain • British phrasebook • Central Europe • Central Europe phrasebook • Croatia • Czech & Slovak Republics • Denmark • Dublin • Eastern Europe • Eastern Europe phrasebook • Edinburgh • Estonia, Latvia & Lithuania • Europe • Finland • France • French phrasebook • Germany • German phrasebook • Greece • Greek phrasebook • Hungary • Iceland, Greenland & the Faroe Islands • Ireland • Italian phrasebook • Italy • Lisbon • London • Mediterranean Europe • Mediterranean Europe phrasebook • Paris • Poland • Portugal • Portugal travel atlas • Prague • Provence & the Côte D'Azur • Romania & Moldova • Russia, Ukraine & Belarus • Russian phrasebook • Scandinavian & Baltic Europe • Scandinavian Europe phrasebook • Scotland • Slovenia • Spain • Spanish phrasebook • St Petersburg • Switzerland • Trekking in Spain • Ukrainian phrasebook • Vienna • Walking in Britain • Walking in Italy • Walking in Ireland • Walking in Switzerland • Western Europe • Western Europe phrasebook
Travel Literature: The Olive Grove: Travels in Greece

INDIAN SUBCONTINENT Bangladesh • Bengali phrasebook • Bhutan • Delhi • Goa • Hindi/Urdu phrasebook • India • India & Bangladesh travel atlas • Indian Himalaya • Karakoram Highway • Nepal • Nepali phrasebook • Pakistan • Rajasthan • South India • Sri Lanka • Sri Lanka phrasebook • Trekking in the Indian Himalaya • Trekking in the Karakoram & Hindukush • Trekking in the Nepal Himalaya